Intr

Welcome to **"Chess Opening** signed to help young chess players like you popular and effective openings for playing with the White pieces.

As you may already know, **the opening** is the first part of the game where each player makes their initial moves to control the board and set up their pieces for the rest of the game. By studying different openings, you can learn how to gain an advantage over your opponent and improve your chances of winning.

In fact, often it is the player with Black pieces, who chooses the opening with his first move, but the player with the White pieces can limit his options. For example, when White starts with the move 1. e4, Black have several good answers (e5, c5, e6, d5), and each of them leads to different chess opening!

The **idea of this book** is to let you quickly try out different openings and see, if you like them or not. This book will give you a solid foundation and help you to develop your chess skills and become a more confident player. So, let's get started and have some fun exploring the exciting world of chess openings!

How to use this book

For each opening you will get a **short history**, **basic ideas**, main order of moves and couple of most popular **variations**. You will be provided with suggestions where to put your **pawns and pieces**, a **model chess game** with this opening by a strong grandmaster or World champion.

You will get four very simple **exercises** to help you memorize the order of moves. Your goal is to find the best move for white, mark it with an arrow and write it down below the diagram. **Solutions** to exercises can be found in each opening's description and also at the end of the book.

Example

2.

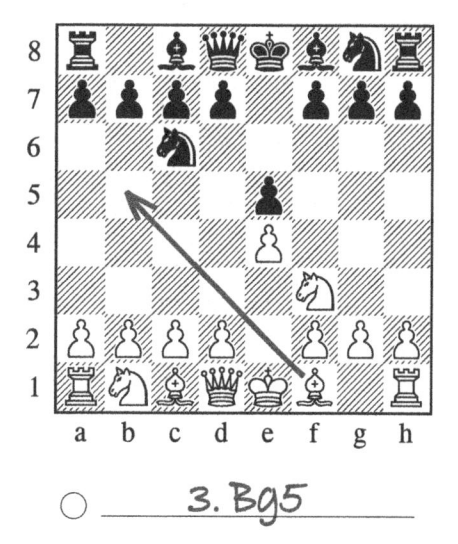

○ _____ 3. Bg5

Ruy Lopez (Spanish Game)

History

The Ruy Lopez is a chess opening that was named after a Spanish bishop named Ruy Lopez de Segura who wrote a book about chess in the 16th century. It is one of the oldest and most popular openings in chess. Many chess players have studied and played this opening throughout history, making it a classic and timeless strategy.

Basic ideas

Ruy Lopez starts with the moves 1. e4 e5 2. ♘f3 ♞c6 3. ♗b5. The basic idea of the opening is to **control the center of the board and develop your pieces quickly**. By moving your bishop to b5, you put pressure on black's knight and gain control of key squares. From there, you can continue to build your position and launch an attack on your opponent's king.

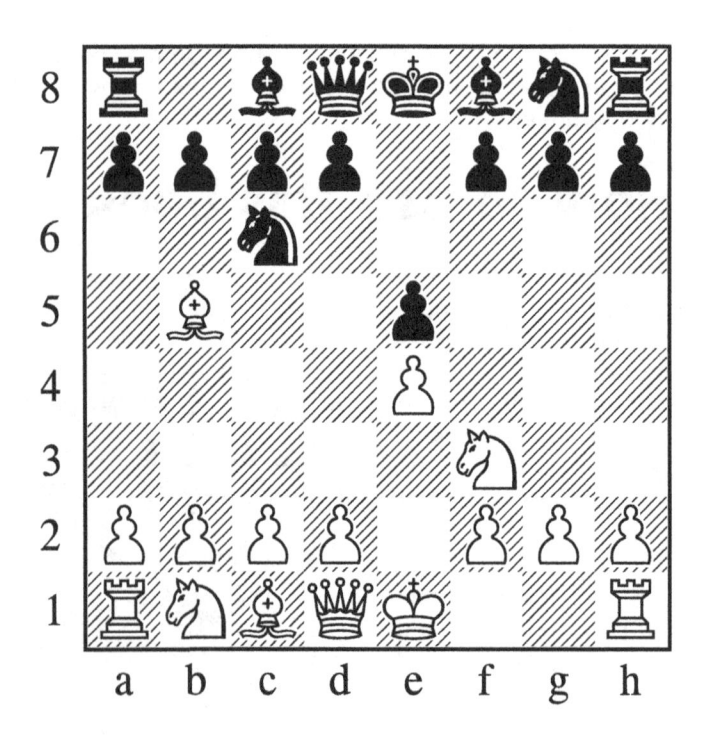

1. e4 e5 2. ♘f3 ♞c6 3. ♗b5

Top variations

Morphy Defense: 3...a6

Most popular third move for Black. White has to decide whether to retreat or to exchange for Black's knight. If you retreat the Bishop to a4, usually after Black's b5 you have to retreat it once again to b3. Then remember to play pawn to c3, not to fall into the Noah's Ark Trap.

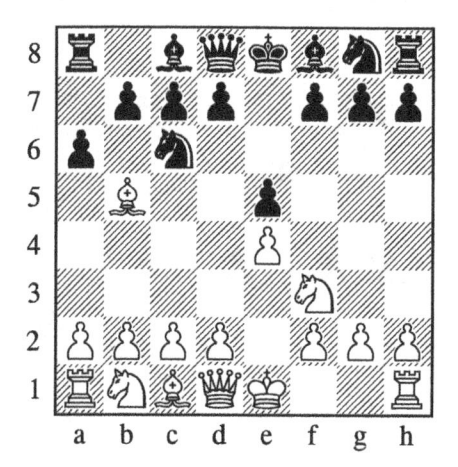

Classical Defense: 3...♝c5

Possibly the oldest defense to the Ruy Lopez, played by former world champion Boris Spassky. White's most common reply is 4. c3.

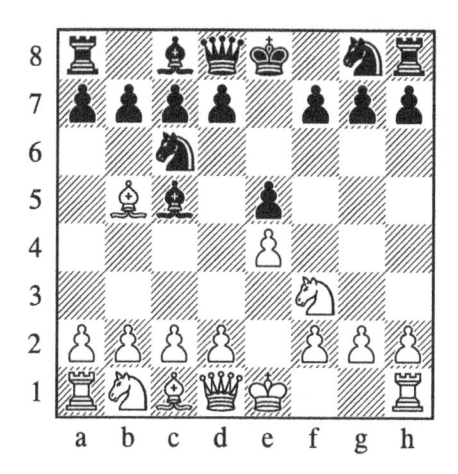

Main line

Ruy Lopez

1. e4 e5 2. ♘f3 ♞c6 3. ♗b5 a6 4. ♗a4 ♞f6 5. O-O ♝e7

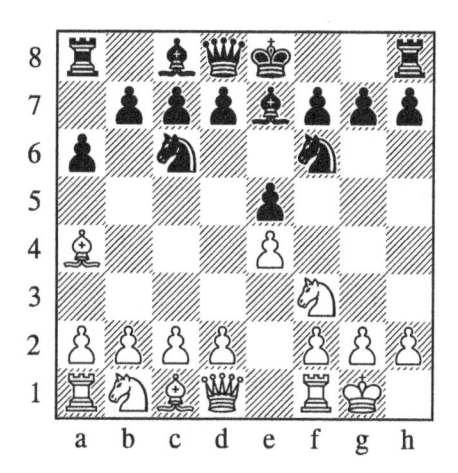

Where to put pawns and pieces

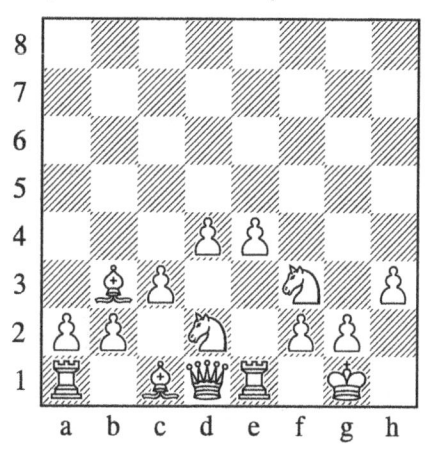

> ### Did you know?
> Common nickname for the opening is "The Spanish Torture" due to difficulty for Black to equalize

Chess Openings for Kids with White

Ruy Lopez (Spanish Game)

Model game

Emanuel Lasker vs Richard Teichmann
St. Petersburg (1909)

1. e4 1...e5 2. ♘f3 ♘c6 3. ♗b5 a6 4. ♗a4 ♘f6 5. O-O ♗e7 6. ♕e2 b5 7. ♗b3 d6 8. c3 O-O

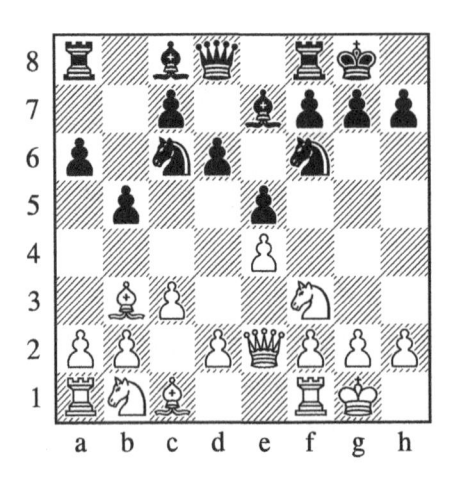

9. d4 exd4 10. cxd4 ♗g4 11. ♖d1 d5 12. e5 ♘e4 13. ♘c3 ♘xc3 14. bxc3 f6?!

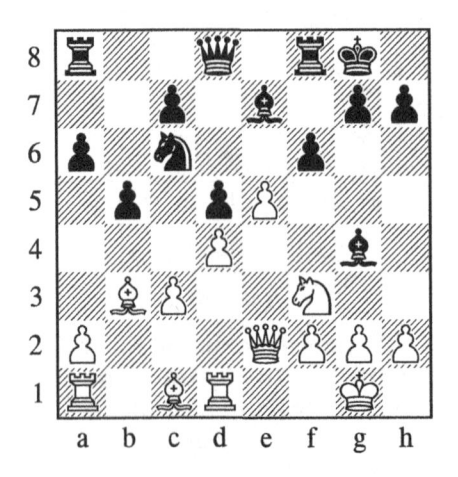

16. g4 ♗f7 17. e6 17...♗g6 18. ♘h4 ♘a5?! 19. ♘xg6 19...hxg6 20. ♗c2 f5?! 21. ♔h1 ♗d6 22. gxf5?! ♕h4 23. ♕f3 gxf5 24. ♖g1

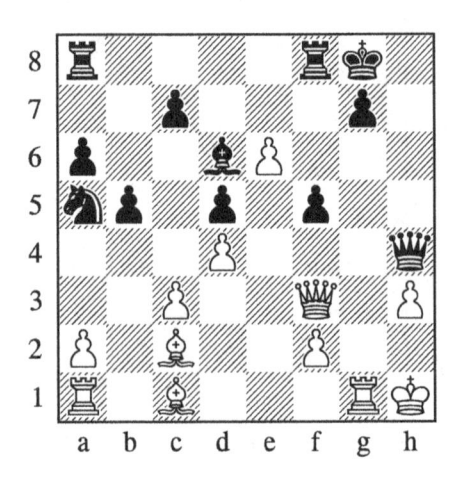

24...f4?? 25. ♖g4 ♕h6 26. e7 ♗xe7 27. ♗xf4 ♕e6?? 1-0

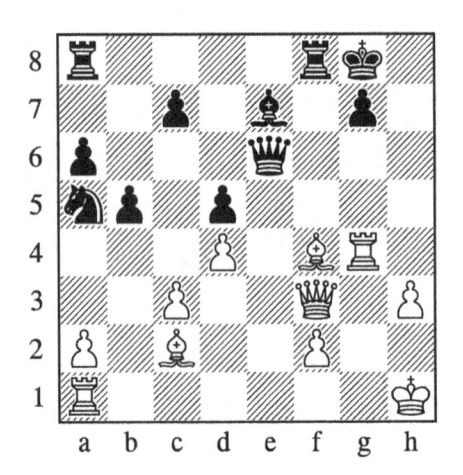

Ruy Lopez (Spanish Game)

Find the best move for White

1.

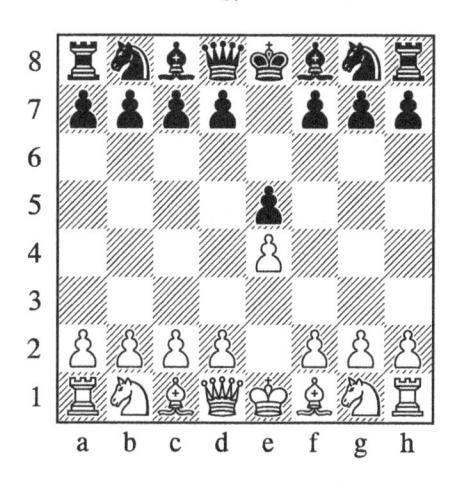

2.

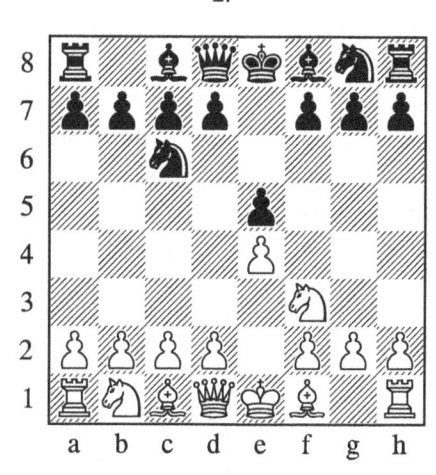

○ _____

○ _____

3.

4.

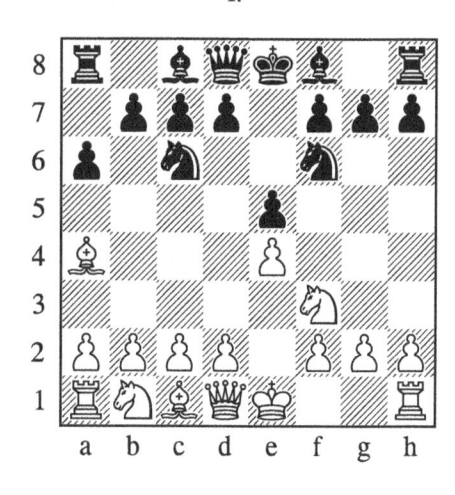

○ _____

○ _____

Italian Game

History

The main variation of Italian Game is called **"Giuoco Piano,"** which means **"quiet game."** This opening was first played by chess players hundreds of years ago, way back in the 16th century. Over time, it became more and more popular, especially in Italy, where it was first developed.

Basic ideas

Italian Game starts with 1. e4 e5 2. ♘f3 ♞c6 3. ♗c4 and allows to **build a strong position** on the board and **prepare for a more aggressive attack later** in the game. Starting with 1. e4 controls the center and opens up the diagonals for the bishop and the queen. White quickly develops the kingside pieces to their best squares. On move four, White is ready to castle.

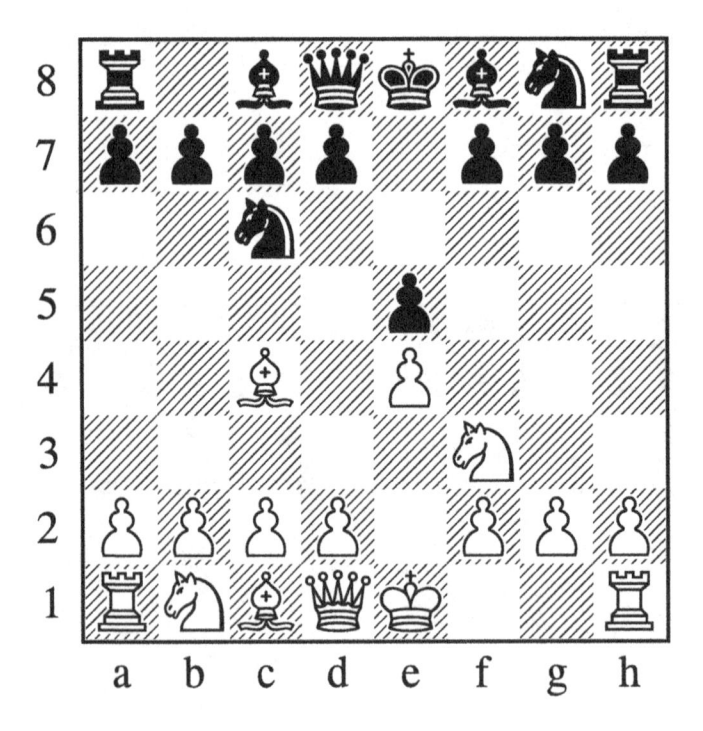

1. e4 e5 2. ♘f3 ♞c6 3. ♗c4

Top variations

Giuoco Pianissimo: 4. d3

Giuoco Pianissimo (Italian: "Very Quiet Game") is the most popular variation. White opens up the bishop and defends e4. By avoiding an immediate confrontation in the centre, White prevents the early release of tension through exchanges and enters a positional maneuvering game.

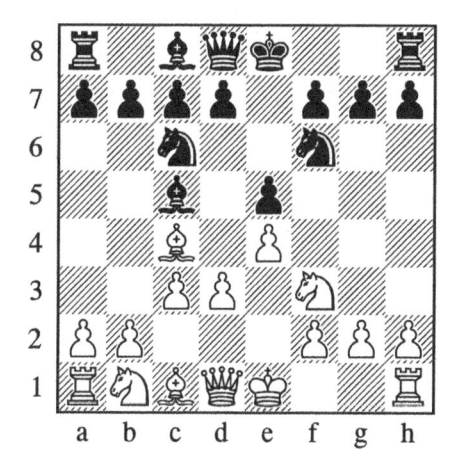

Two Knights Defense 3...♘f6

Black's third move (instead of ♗c5) is a more aggressive defense than the Giuoco Piano.

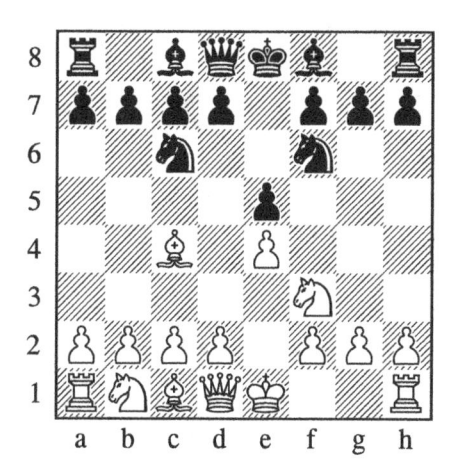

Main line

Giuoco Piano

1. e4 e5 2. ♘f3 ♘c6 3. ♗c4 ♗c5 4. c3 ♘f6 5. d4 exd4 6. cxd4

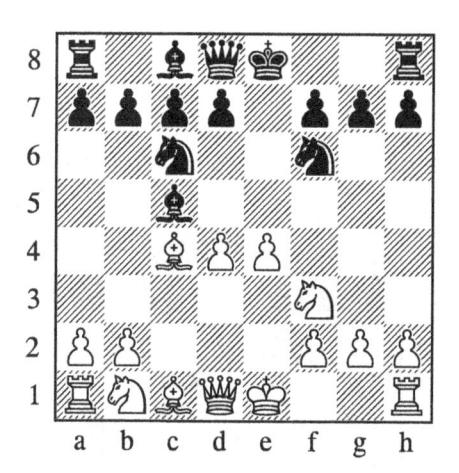

Where to put pawns and pieces

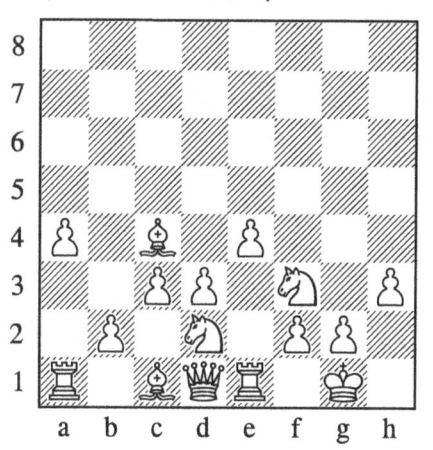

Did you know?

The Italian Game is one of the oldest recorded chess openings – it occurs in the "Göttingen manuscript" (1471)

Chess Openings for Kids with White

Italian Game

Model game

Garry Kasparov vs Agnelo Queiroz
Sao Paolo (2004)

1. e4 e5 2. ♘f3 ♞c6 3. ♗c4 ♝c5
4. c3 ♞f6 5. d3 d6 6. ♗b3 ♝g4

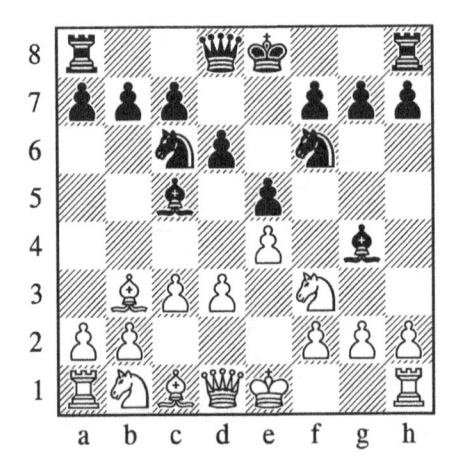

7. h3 ♝h5 8. ♘bd2 O-O 9. ♕e2 a6 10. ♘f1 h6? 11. g4 ♝g6 12. ♘g3 ♞e7?

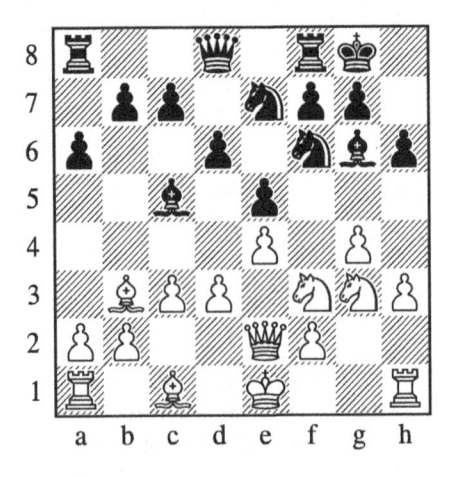

13. ♘h4 ♞h7 14. ♘hf5 ♝xf5 15. gxf5 ♞f6? 16. ♖g1 ♚h8 17. ♘h5 ♞xh5?! 18. ♕xh5 ♞g8

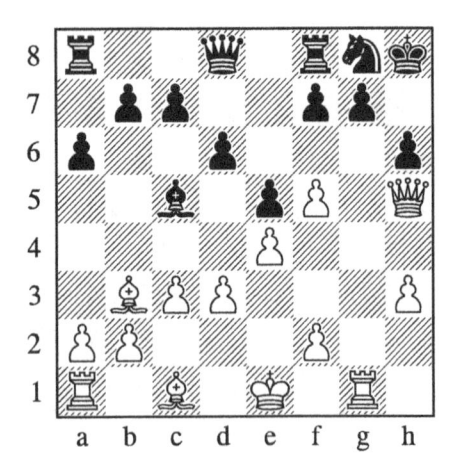

19. ♗xf7 ♕f6 20. ♗b3 c6 21. ♖g6 ♕e7 22. ♗xg8 ♖xg8 23. ♗g5 1-0

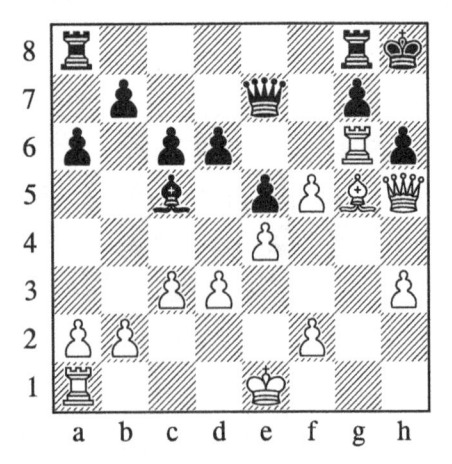

Black resigned, as he either loses his queen or gets checkmated.

Italian Game

Find the best move for White

5.

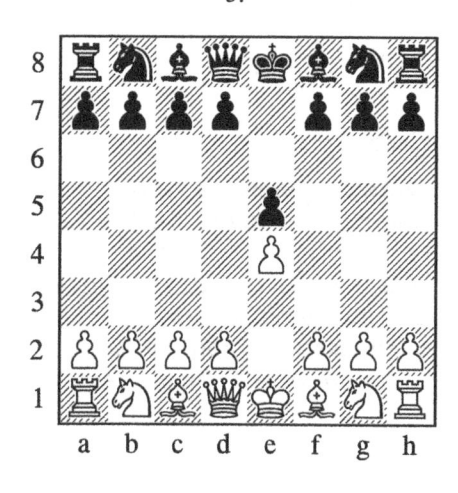

6.

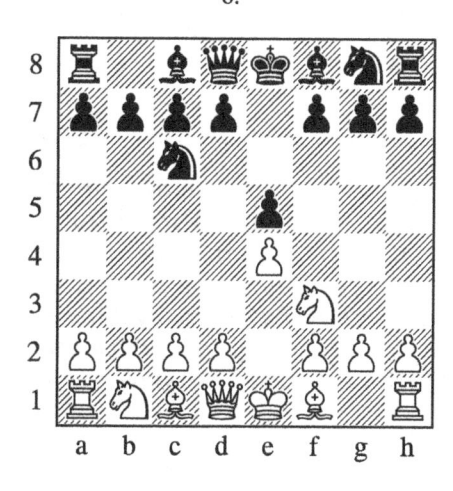

○ _____

○ _____

7.

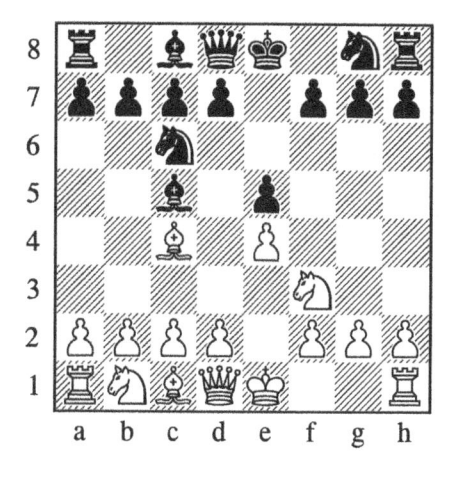

8.

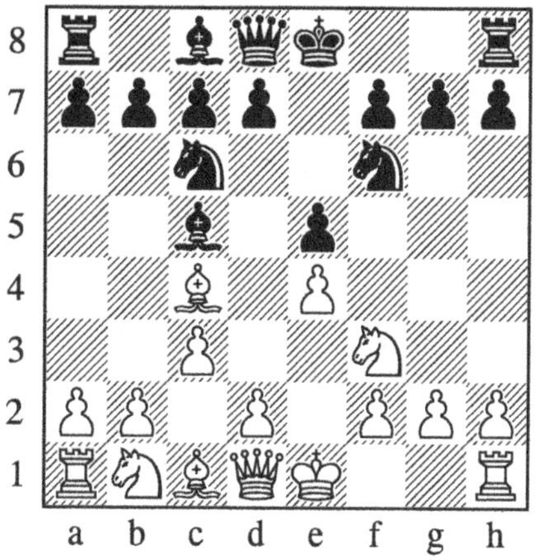

○ _____

○ _____

Queen's Gambit

History

Queen's Gambit is a chess opening that has been played by chess players for over 150 years. It gets its name from the move **"gambit"**, which means that one player gives up a pawn in order to gain an advantage. Some of the greatest players of all time, such as Bobby Fischer and Garry Kasparov, have used the Queen's Gambit in their games.

Basic ideas

By playing the moves d4 and c4, white **puts pawns in the center of the board**, which can help control more squares. Black can take the pawn on c4 with their own pawn, but doing so can lead to some disadvantages, such as losing control of the center of the board. The Queen's Gambit can lead to many different types of positions, depending on how both players respond. **White's focus is on developing their pieces**, while Black tries to attack White's position or gain control of the center.

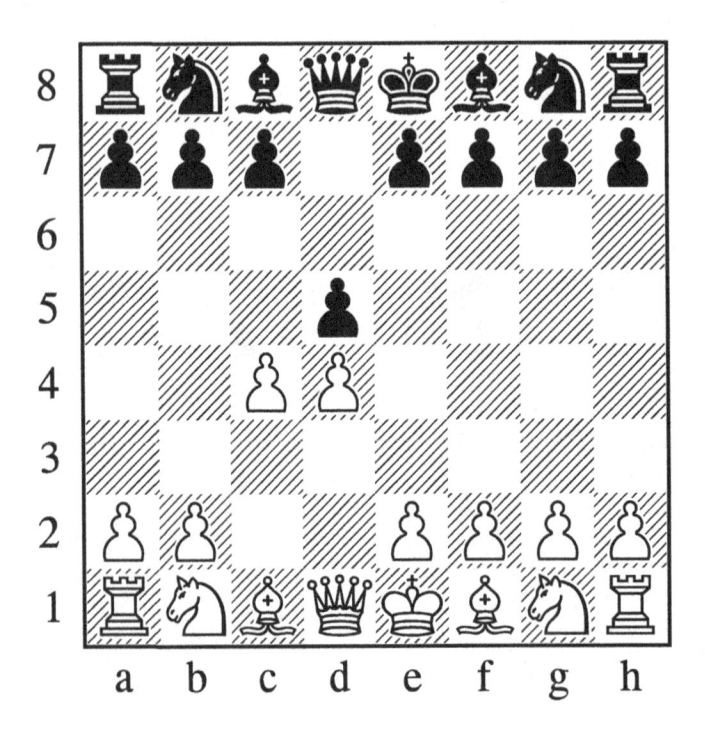

1. d4 d5 2. c4

Top variations

Queen's Gambit Accepted: 2...dxc4

The Queen's Gambit is not considered a true gambit, because the pawn can only be held unprofitably by Black. Black usually allows the pawn to be recaptured, and uses the time expended to play against White's centre. White continues with moves like ♘f3, e4 or e3.

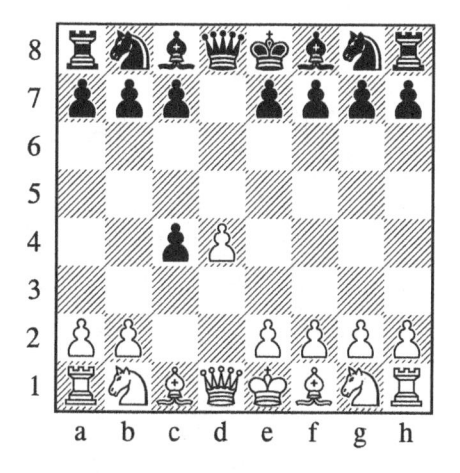

Slav Defense: 2...c6

The Slav is one of the primary defenses to the Queen's Gambit. White plays ♘f3 here.

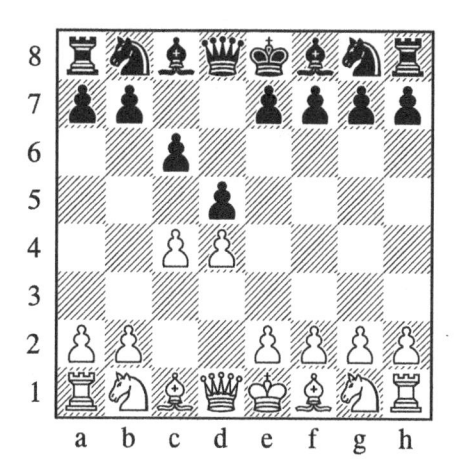

Main line

Queen's Gambit Declined

1. d4 d5 2. c4 e6 3. ♘f3 ♞f6 4. ♘c3

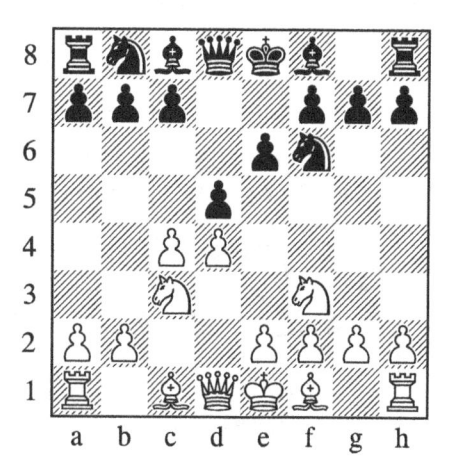

Where to put pawns and pieces

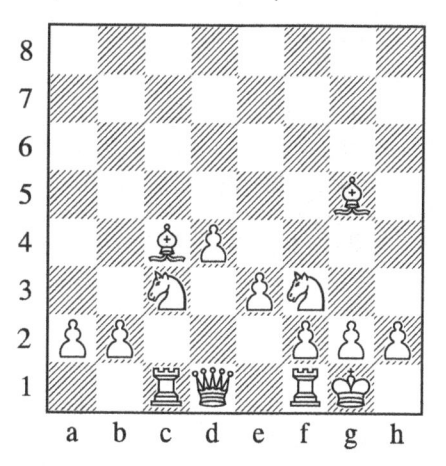

Did you know?

In recent years, the Queen's Gambit has gained even more popularity thanks to the Netflix series "The Queen's Gambit"

Chess Openings for Kids with White

Queen's Gambit

Model game

Robert James Fischer vs Boris Spassky
Reykjavik (1972)

1. c4 e6 2. ♘f3 d5 3. d4 ♘f6 4. ♘c3 ♗e7 5. ♗g5 O-O 6. e3 h6

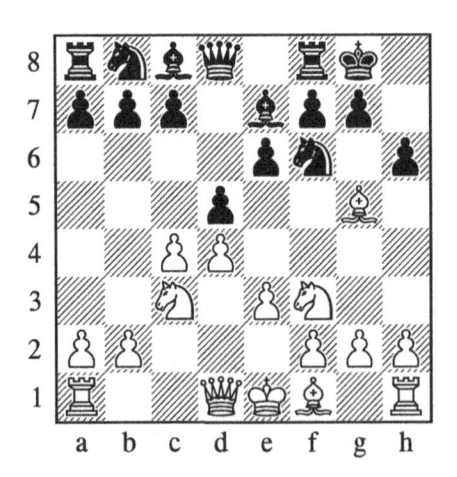

7. ♗h4 b6 8. cxd5 ♘xd5 9. ♗xe7 ♕xe7 10. ♘xd5 exd5 11. ♖c1 ♗e6 12. ♕a4 c5 13. ♕a3 ♖c8 14. ♗b5 a6 15. dxc5 bxc5 16. O-O ♖a7 17. ♗e2 ♘d7 18. ♘d4 ♕f8 19. ♘xe6 fxe6 20. e4 d4 21. f4 ♕e7 22. e5 ♖b8??

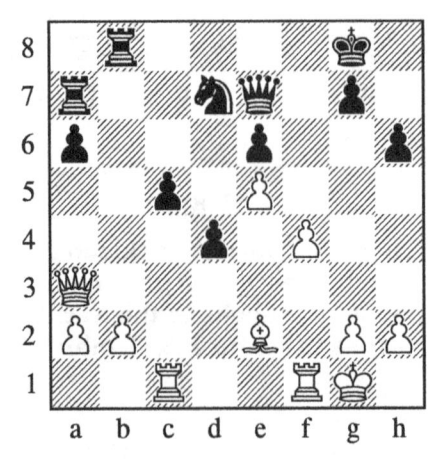

23. ♗c4 ♔h8 24. ♕h3 ♘f8 25. b3 a5 26. f5 exf5 27. ♖xf5 ♘h7? 28. ♖cf1 ♕d8 29. ♕g3 ♖e7 30. h4 ♖bb7 31. e6

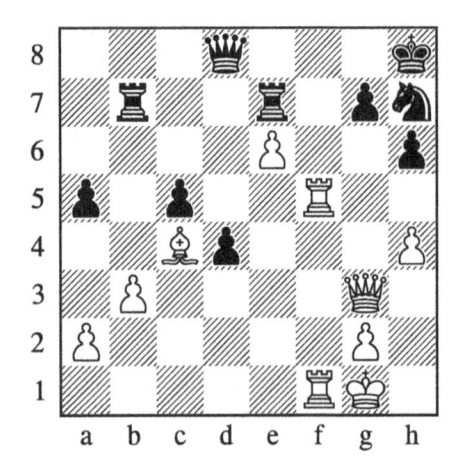

31...♕e6 32. ♖bc7 32. ♕e5 ♕e8 33. a4 ♕d8 34. ♖1f2 ♕e8 35. ♖2f3 ♕d8 36. ♗d3 ♕e8?? 37. ♕e4 ♘f6 38. ♖xf6 gxf6 39. ♖xf6 ♔g8 40. ♗c4 ♔h8? 41. ♕f4 1-0

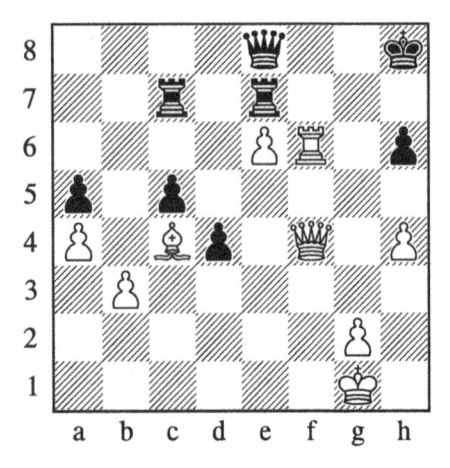

Chess Openings for Kids with White

Queen's Gambit

Find the best move for White

9.

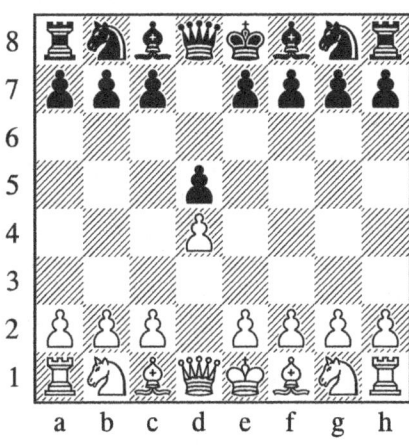

10.

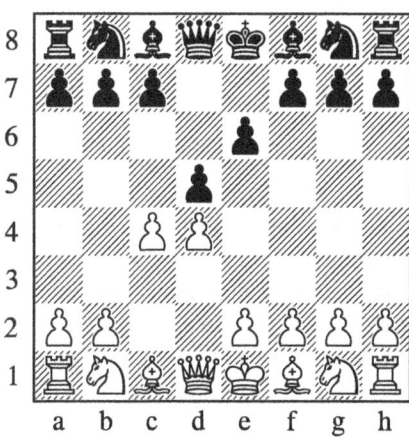

○ _____

○ _____

11.

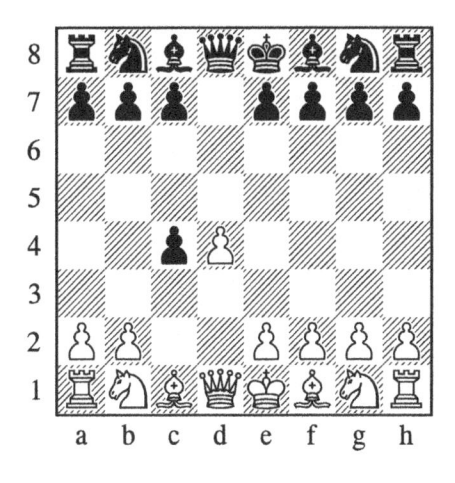

12.

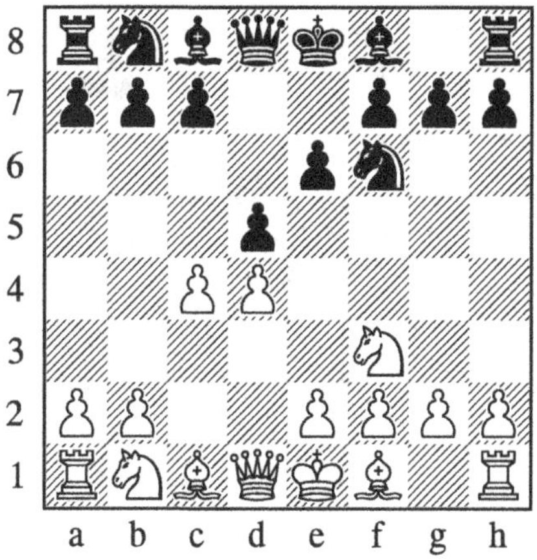

○ _____

○ _____

Sicilian Defense

History

The **Sicilian Defense** is named after the Italian island of **Sicily**, which was a center of Greek and Roman culture and history. The opening is believed to have originated in the 16th century, but it was not until the 20th century that it became widely popular and recognized as a powerful weapon for black.

Basic ideas

By advancing the c-pawn at the first move, Black creates an asymmetry in the pawn structure. The key ideas for white in the Sicilian Defense are to **control the center, quickly develop your pieces, prepare for a counterattack,** and be familiar with the different variations of the opening. Black usually attacks on the queenside and White on the kingside. Often both sides castle in opposite directions and begin direct attack with pawns and pieces on the opponent's king.

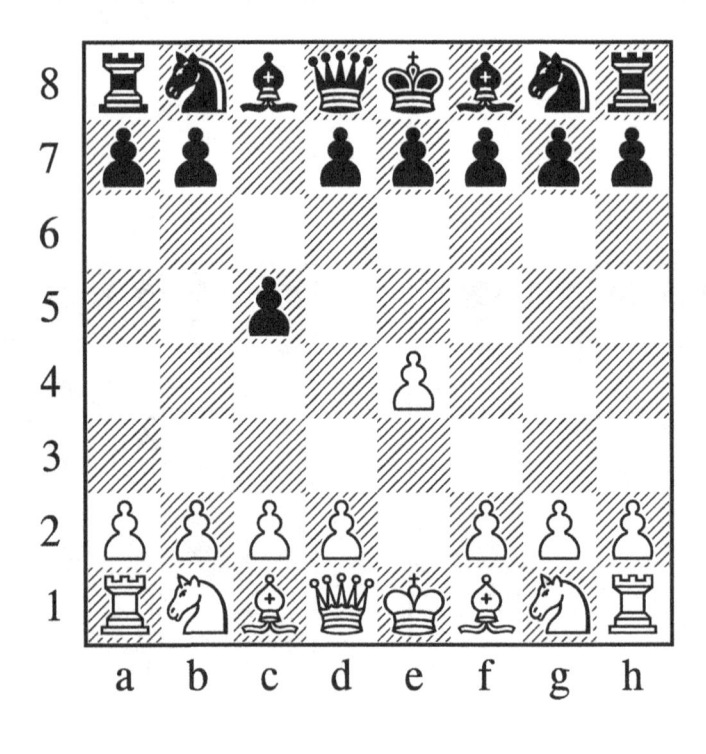

1. e4 c5

Top variations

Open Sicilian: 2. ♘f3 and 3. d4

White plays a quick ♘f3 and d4 and attempts to open the position to take advantage of Black's slow development. Most popular Open Sicilian variation is Najdorf.

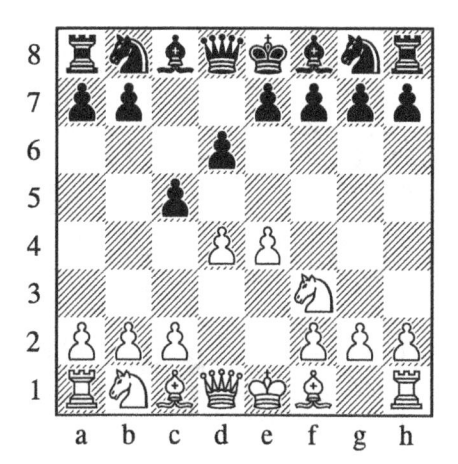

Closed Sicilian: 2. ♘c3

The Closed Sicilian is a variation of the Sicilian Defense in which White doesn't open the center with an early d2-d4. Instead, White often fianchettos the light-squared bishop and plans to slowly build up on the kingside.

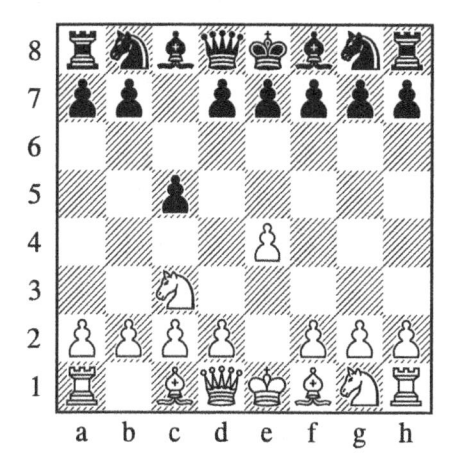

Main line

Classical Variation

1. e4 c5 2. ♘f3 ♘c6 3. d4 cxd4 4. ♘xd4 ♘f6 5. ♘c3 d6.

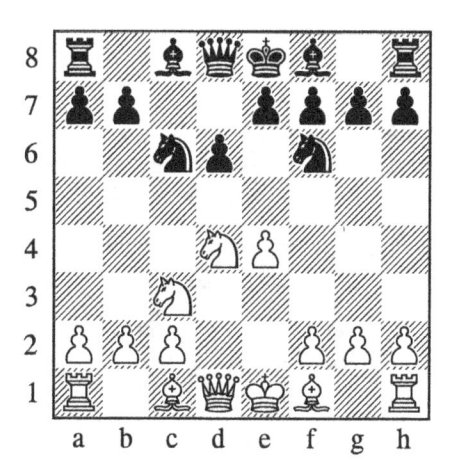

Where to put pawns and pieces

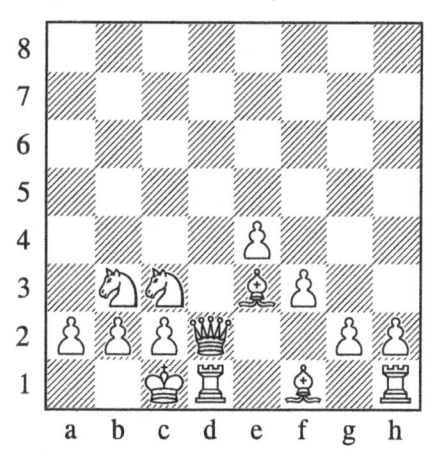

Did you know?

It is statistically proven that Sicilian Defense is the best method of responding to 1. e4. It has shown a win rate for White of just 52.3%.

Chess Openings for Kids with White

Sicilian Defense

Model game

Mikhail Tal vs Fridrik Olafsson
Zagreb (1959)

1. e4 c5 2. ♘f3 d6 3. d4 cxd4 4. ♘xd4 ♞f6 5. ♘c3 a6 6. ♗g5 e6 7. f4 h6 8. ♗h4 ♛b6 9. a3 ♞c6

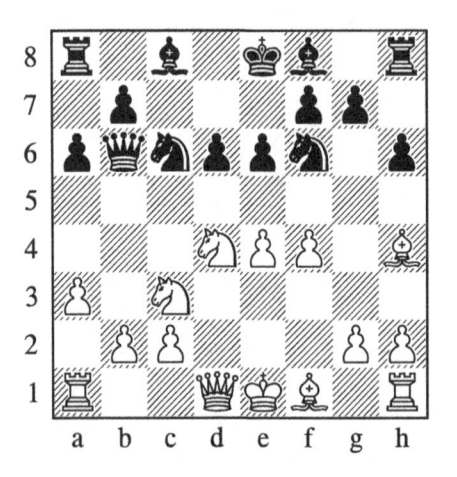

10. ♗f2 ♛c7 11. ♕f3 ♝e7 12. 0-0-0 ♝d7 13. g4 g5 14. ♘xc6 ♝xc6 15. fxg5 hxg5 16. ♗d4 ♜h6 17. h4 ♞d7 18. h5 ♛a5?! 19. ♗e2 b5 20. ♜hf1 f6 21. ♘a2 ♛c7 22. ♕b3 ♚f7 23. ♕e3 ♜g8 24. ♔b1 ♞e5

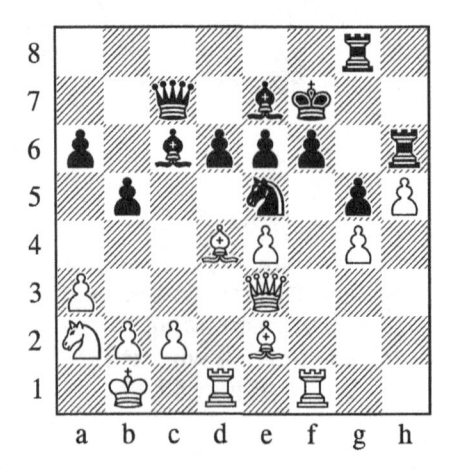

25. ♘c3 ♛g7 26. ♜d2 ♜b8 27. ♜fd1 ♝e8 28. ♘a2 a5 29. ♕c3 ♛xc3 30. ♗xc3 ♜a8 31. b4 ♝c6 32. bxa5 ♝xe4 33. ♗b4 ♚f7 34. ♘c3 ♝c6 35. ♘xb5 ♝xb5 36. ♗xb5 d5?

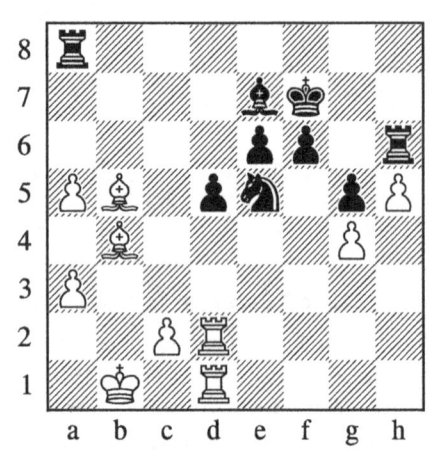

37. c4 ♜b8 38. a6 ♜hh8 39. ♔a2 ♝xb4 40. axb4 dxc4 41. ♜d7+ ♘xd7 42. ♜xd7+ ♚f8 43. a7 1-0

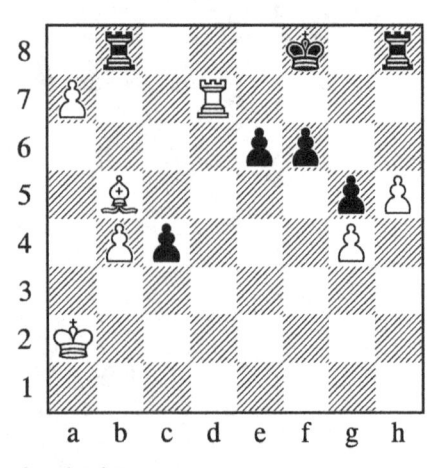

16 *Chess Openings for Kids with White*

Sicilian Defense

Find the best move for White

13.

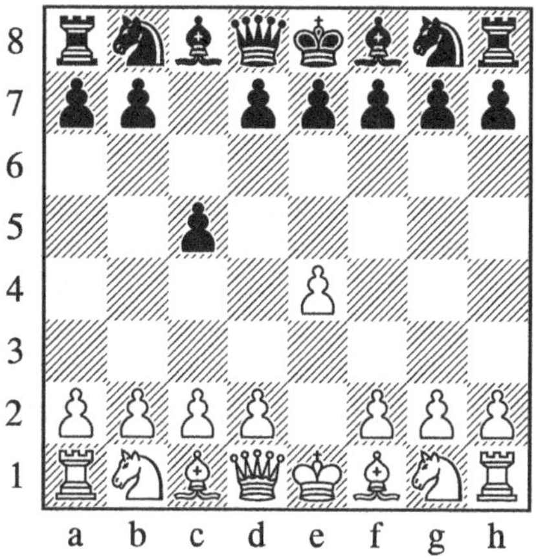

○ _____

14.

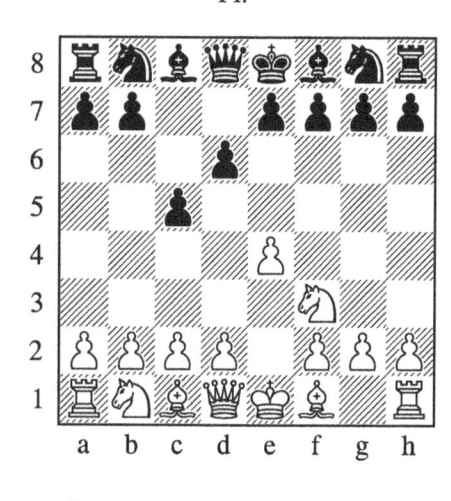

○ _____

15.

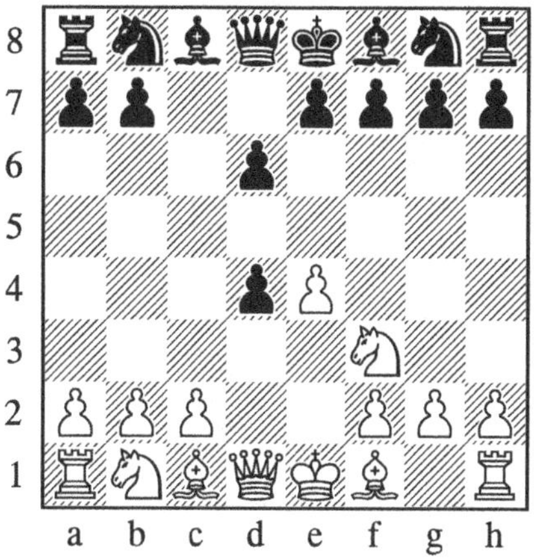

○ _____

16.

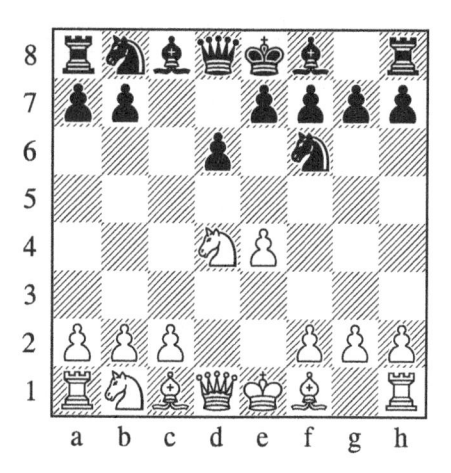

○ _____

English Opening

History

The **English Opening** is a flank opening and it is the fourth most popular and one of the four most successful of White's twenty possible first moves. Opening got its name from the leading 19th century English master Howard Staunton, who played it during 1843 match. It is now recognised as a solid opening thatmany World champions have played.

Basic ideas

With the pawn move 1. c4 White immediately grabs some **central space** and takes the d5 square under control. The c-pawn does a good job of controlling center, while allowing White to remain flexible in the deployment of their two central pawns. This **flexibility** allows White to adapt their strategy according to their opponent's responses. This opening often leads to a position where White has **more pieces aimed at Black's kingside**. This can create a lot of pressure on Black's position and give White attacking opportunities.

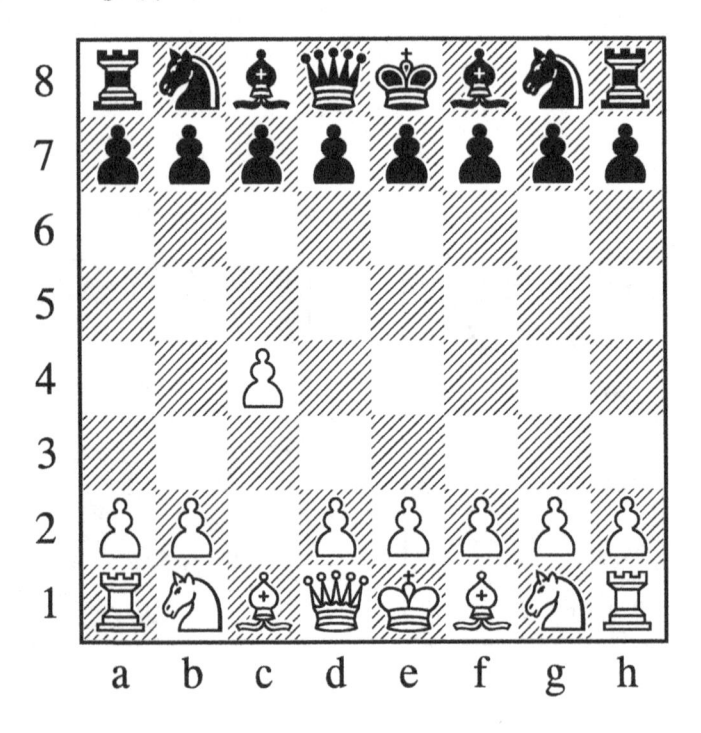

1. c4

Top variations

Symmetrical Defense: 1...c5

The Symmetrical Defense is named so because both of the c-pawns are advanced two squares, maintaining symmetry. White can continue with moves like ♘f3, ♘c3 or g3 and fianchetto the bishop to g2.

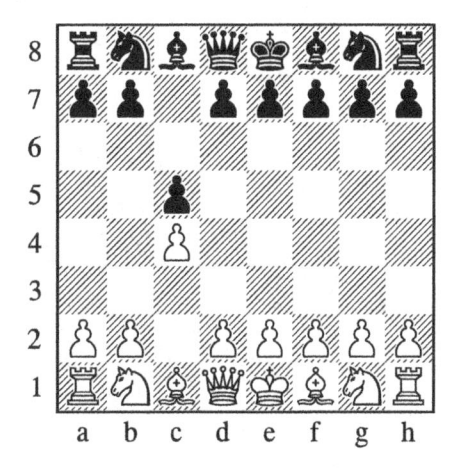

Reversed Sicilian: 1...e5

After 1...e5, White has Black's position in the Sicilian but with an extra tempo. This is often called the Reversed Sicilian. White usually continues his development with ♘c3, ♘f3, g3 and ♗g2.

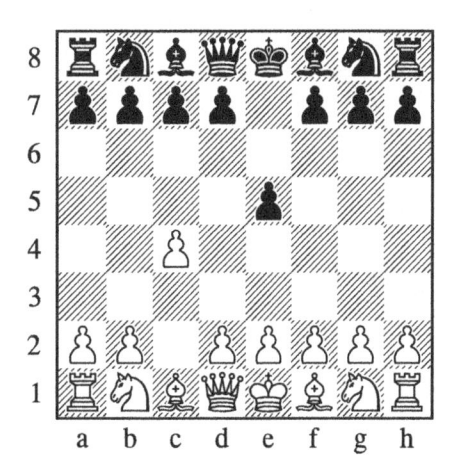

Main line

Classical Variation

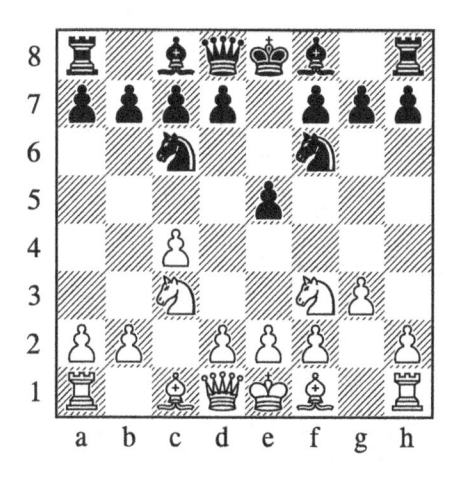

1. c4 e5 2. ♘c3 ♞f6 3. ♘f3 ♞c6 4. g3

Where to put pawns and pieces

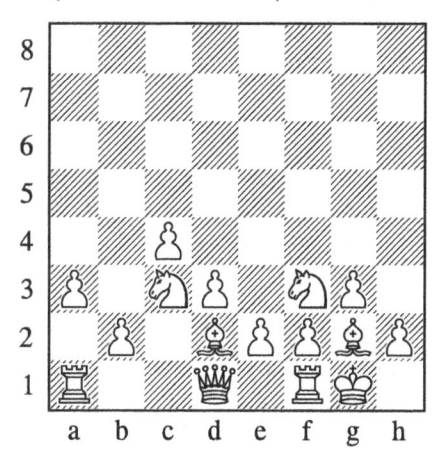

Did you know?

Howard Staunton's contemporaries where not impressed by English Opening. The Opening caught on only in the twentieth century.

Chess Openings for Kids with White

English Opening

Model game

Magnus Carlsen vs Anish Giri
Shamkir (2019)

1. c4 e5 2. ♘c3 ♘f6 3. ♘f3 ♘c6 4. g3 d5 5. cxd5 ♘xd5 6. ♗g2 ♗c5 7. 0-0 0-0 8. d3 h6

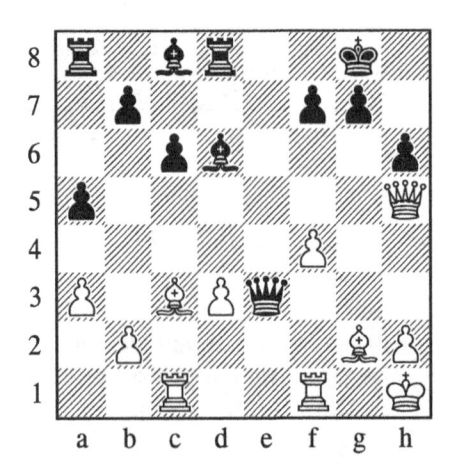

20. ♖ce1 ♕c5 21. f5 ♗f8 22. ♗e4 ♖d5 23. ♖f3 b5 24. ♖g1 ♖a7 25. ♗f6 g6 26. ♕h3?

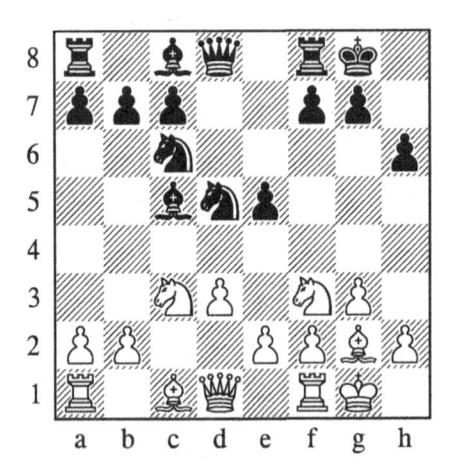

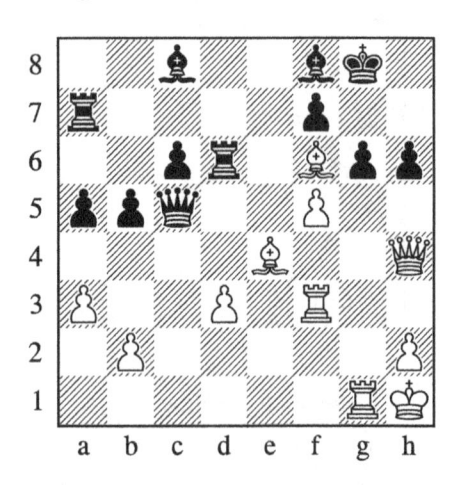

9. ♘xd5 ♕xd5 10. a3 a5 11. ♗d2 ♕e6 12. ♖c1 ♕e7 13. ♗c3 ♘d4 14. e3 ♘xf3+ 15. ♕xf3 ♗d6 16. ♕h5 c6 17. f4 exf4 18. gxf4 ♕xe3+ 19. ♔h1 ♖d8?

26...♖d6 27. ♕h4 ♖xf6 28. ♕xf6 ♗e7 29. ♕xc6 ♕xc6 30. ♗xc6 ♔g7 31. fxg6 fxg6 32. d4 a4 33. d5 b4 34. ♗e8 ♗g5 35. h4 ♗xh4 36. ♖xg6+ ♔h7 37. ♖c6 ♗g4 38. ♖f4 ♖g7 1-0

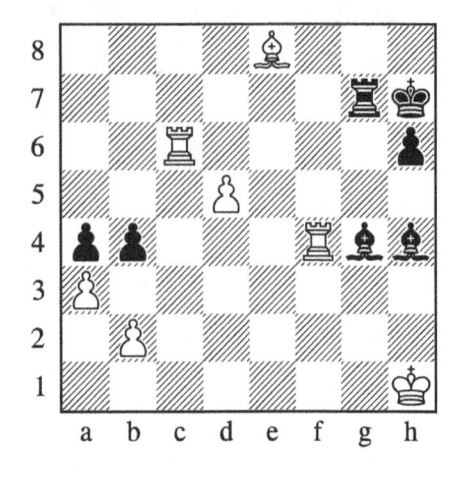

English Opening

Find the best move for White

17.

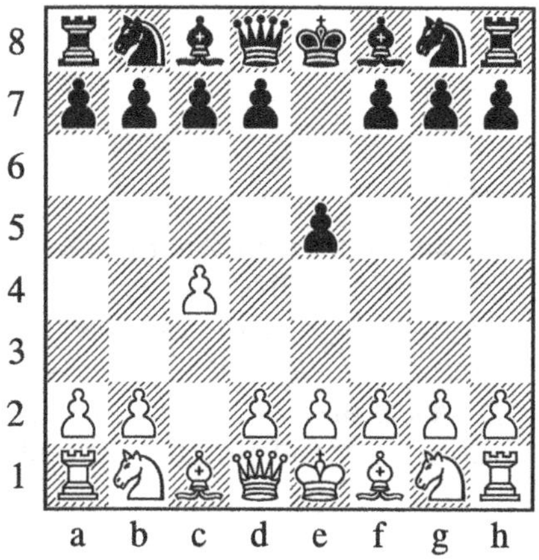

○ _____

18.

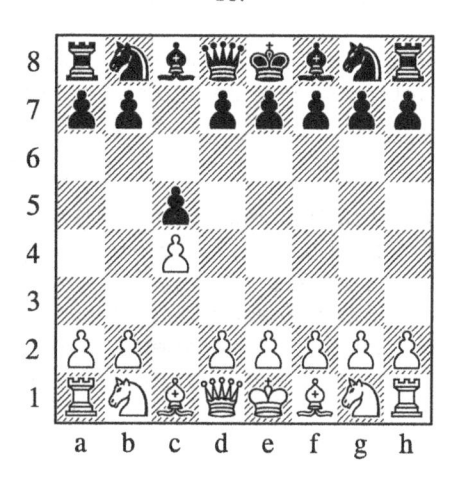

○ _____

19.

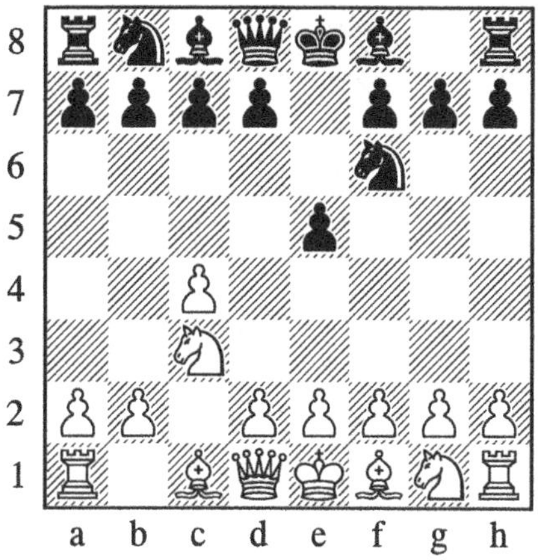

○ _____

20.

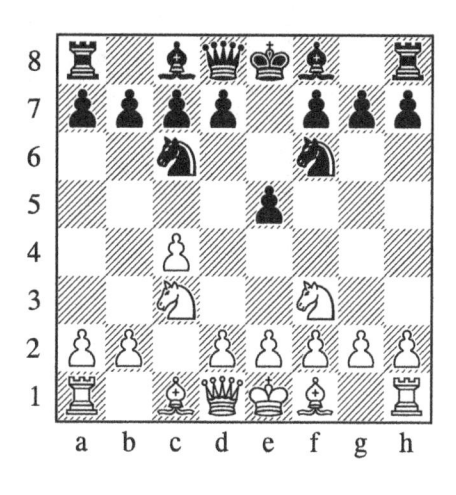

○ _____

Réti Opening

History

The **Réti Opening** is a chess opening named after a famous chess player from Czechoslovakia, **Richard Réti**. The Réti Opening became popular in the early 20th century when Richard Réti used it successfully in his games against strong opponents. Today, it is still played by many chess players and can be a good choice for those who want to surprise their opponents with an unusual opening.

Basic ideas

The basic idea behind the Réti Opening is to **delay committing the pawns in the center of the board**, giving White more **flexibility** to respond to Black's moves. By doing so, White can avoid some of the common defenses that Black may play against other openings. With the move ♘f3 followed by the fianchetto, White **doesn't create any weaknesses** in his camp and it is only after castle that he would start fighting for the center.

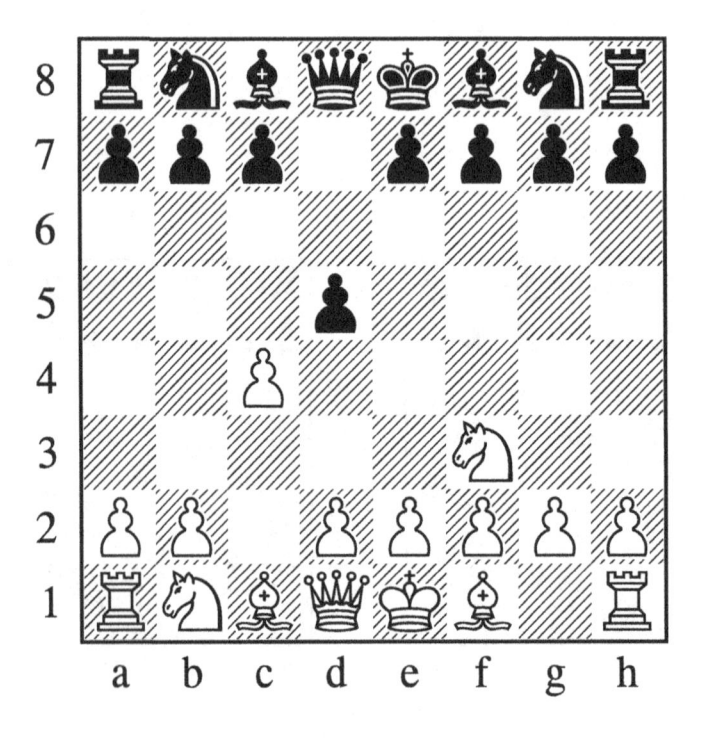

1. ♘f3 d5 2. c4

Top variations

Advancing the Pawn: 2...d4

This gives Black a spatial advantage in the center and a quite annoying pawn on d4. From here, White challenges the pawn with e3, a3 (followed by b4), and b4, while Black tries to hold onto the pawn.

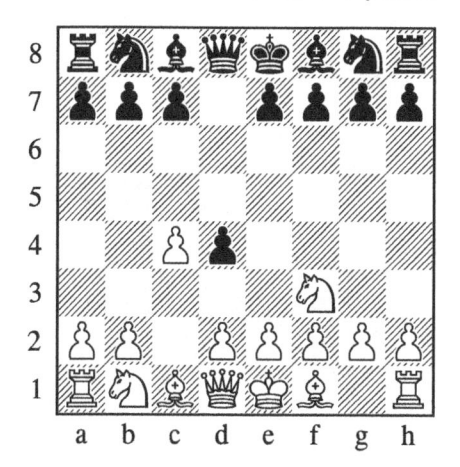

Capturing the Pawn: 2...dxc4

If Black takes the pawn, then in the same manner as in the Queens Gambit Accepted, 3. e3 or 3. e4 regains the pawn with a slight advantage to White, as Black is left somewhat undeveloped.

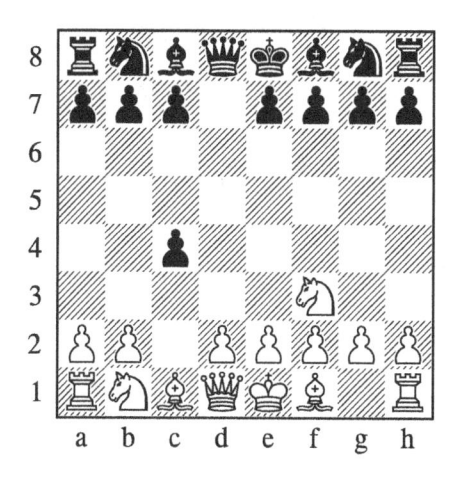

Main line

Defending the Pawn: 2...c6

1. ♘f3 d5 2. c4 c6 3. e3 ♘f6 4. ♘c3 e6 5. b3

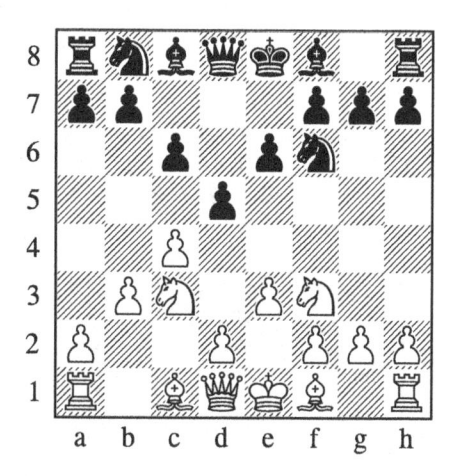

Where to put pawns and pieces

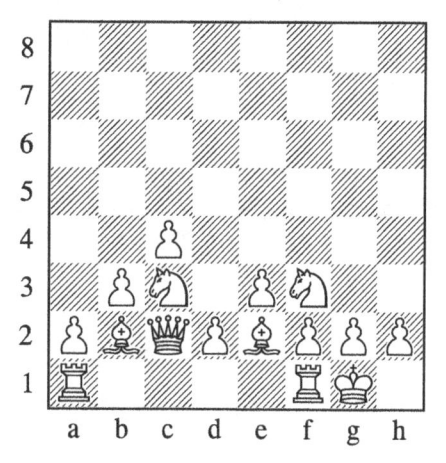

Did you know?

Réti with his opening defeated World Champion José Raúl Capablanca in the New York 1924 chess tournament – Capablanca's first defeat in eight years

Réti Opening

Model game

Richard Réti vs José Raúl Capablanca
New York (1924)

1. ♘f3 ♘f6 2. c4 g6 3. b4 ♗g7 4. ♗b2 O-O 5. g3 b6 6. ♗g2 ♗b7 7. O-O d6 8. d3 ♘bd7 9. ♘bd2 e5 10. ♕c2 ♖e8

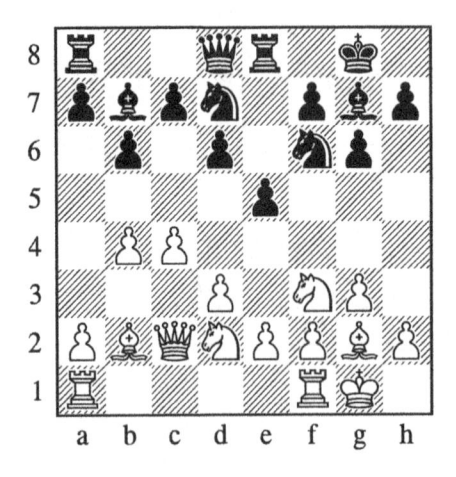

11. ♖fd1 a5 12. a3 h6 13. ♘f1 c5 14. b5 ♘f8 15. e3 ♕c7 16. d4 ♗e4 17. ♕c3 exd4 18. exd4 ♘6d7 19. ♕d2 cxd4 20. ♗xd4 ♕xc4?

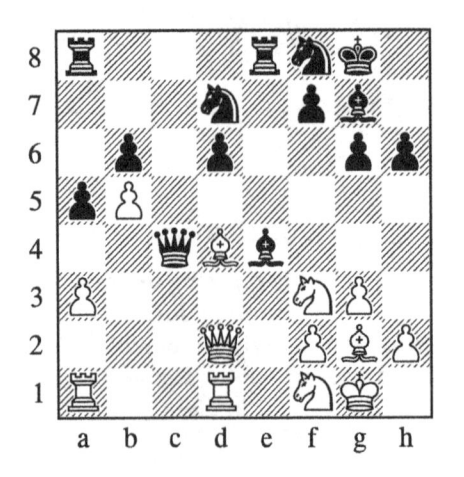

21. ♗xg7 ♔xg7 22. ♕b2+ ♔g8 23. ♖xd6 ♕c5 24. ♖ad1 ♖a7 25. ♘e3 ♕h5 26. ♘d4 ♗xg2 27. ♔xg2 ♕e5?

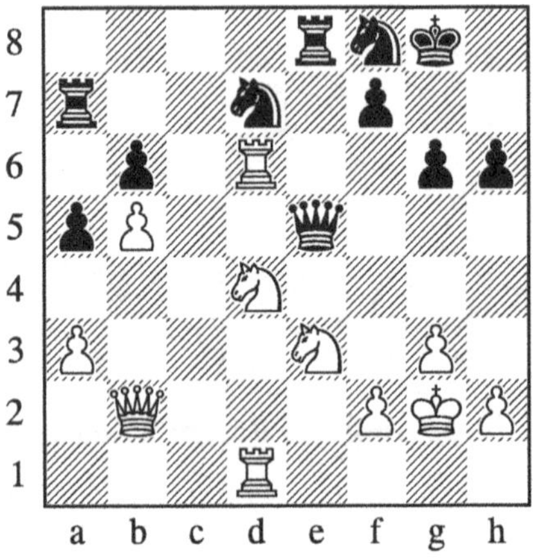

28. ♘c4 ♕c5 29. ♘c6 ♖c7 30. ♘e3 ♘e5 31. ♖1d5 1-0

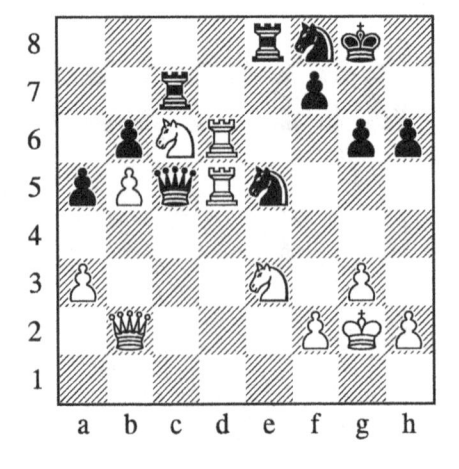

Chess Openings for Kids with White

Réti Opening

Find the best move for White

21.

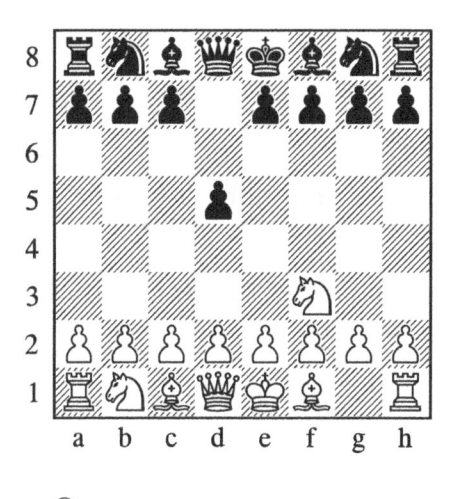

22.

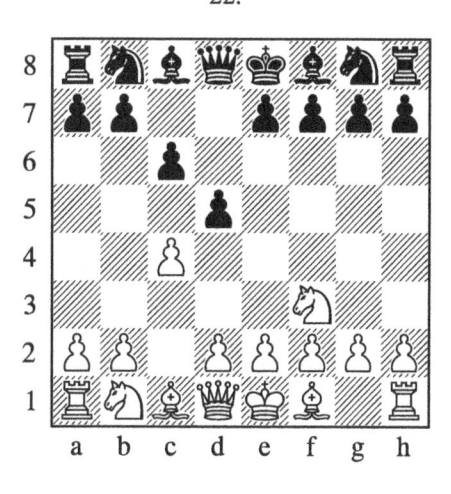

○ _____

○ _____

23.

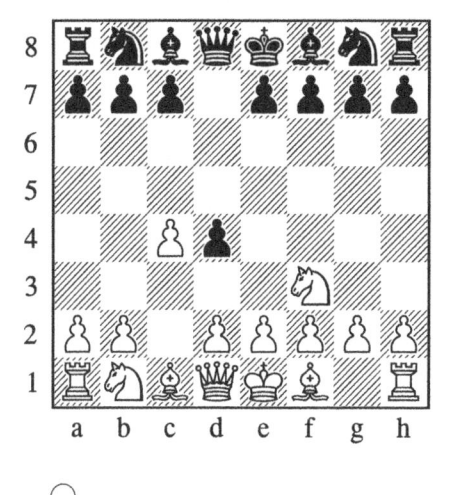

24.

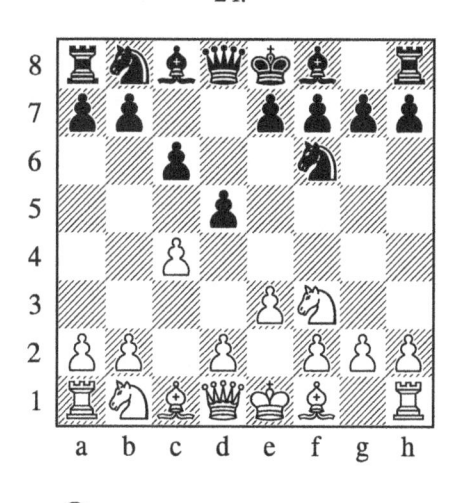

○ _____

○ _____

King's Indian Attack

History

The **King's Indian Attack** (or **KIA**), also known as the **Barcza System** (after Gedeon Barcza), is a chess opening system for White. It has been around for a long time, but it really became popular in the 1950s and 1960s, when a lot of top players started using it. Some of the most famous chess players who have used the King's Indian Attack include Bobby Fischer, Anatoly Karpov, and Garry Kasparov.

Basic ideas

The opening is not a series of specific moves, but rather a **system** that can be played from many different move orders. The idea behind the King's Indian Attack is to **control the center** of the board with your pawns and pieces, and then **attack your opponent's king with your pieces**. It can be a **very aggressive opening** if played correctly, and it's a good choice for players who like to play attacking chess. It's also relatively easy to learn, which is why it's a good choice for younger players.

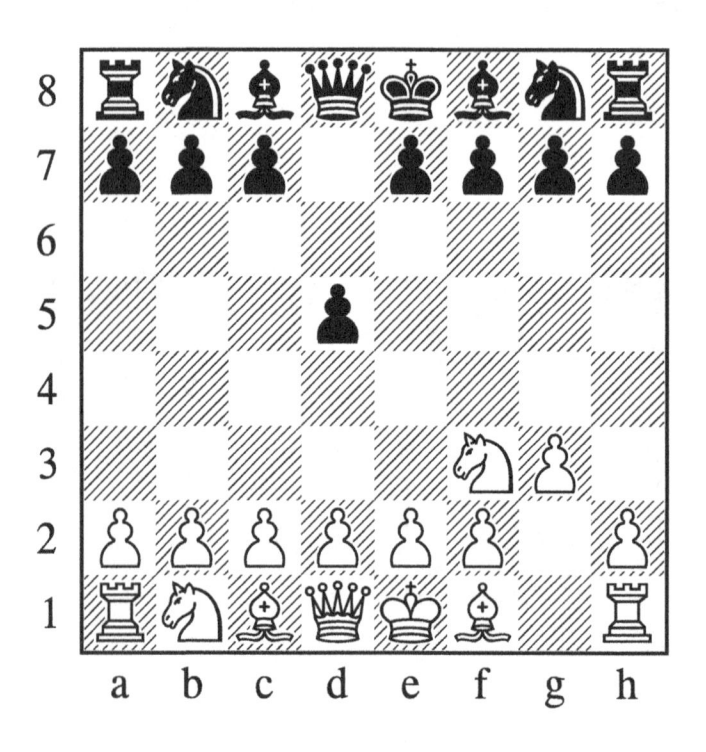

1. ♘f3 d5 2. g3

Top variations

King's Indian Attack: 2...c5

This move gives Black a spatial advantage in the center. White will fianchetto light-squared bishop to g2, castle quickly and then attack the Black's center.

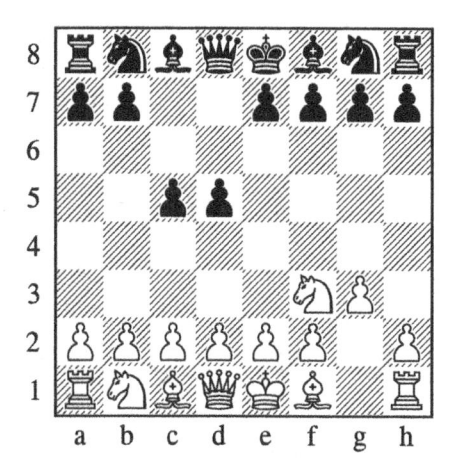

Keres Variation: 2...♗g4

It's a more aggressive approach by Black. After 3. ♗g2 ♘d7 White has several options – he can either play quietly with pawn to d3 and ♘bd2, or grab the center with pawn moves d4 and c4.

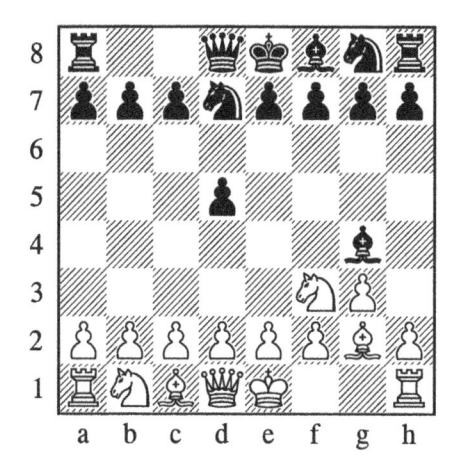

Main line

Barcza System

1. ♘f3 d5 2. g3 ♘f6 3. ♗g2 c6 4. O-O ♗g4 5. d3

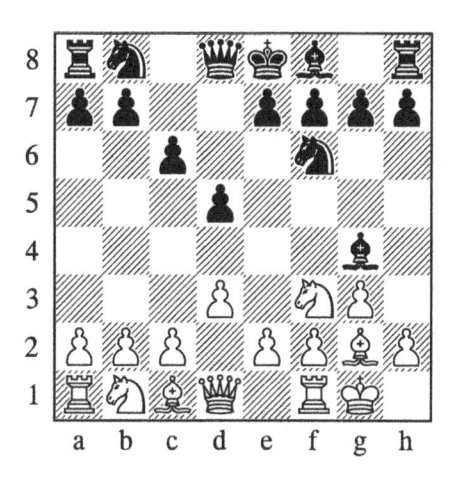

Where to put pawns and pieces

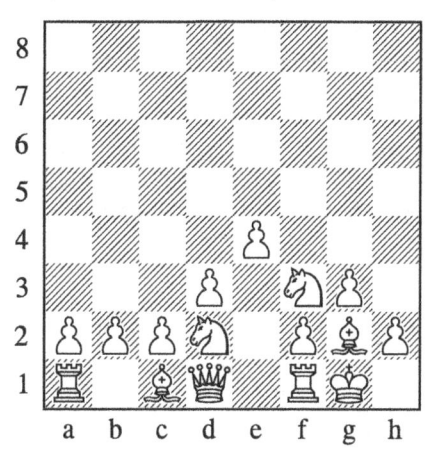

Did you know?

This attacking style is often called a "minority attack," because it involves using your bishops and knights to attack your opponent's stronger pieces.

Chess Openings for Kids with White

King's Indian Attack

Model game

Robert James Fischer vs Lhamsuren Myagmarsuren
Sousse (1967)

1. e4 e6 2. d3 d5 3. ♘d2 ♘f6 4. g3 c5 5. ♗g2 ♘c6 6. ♘gf3 ♗e7 7. 0-0 0-0

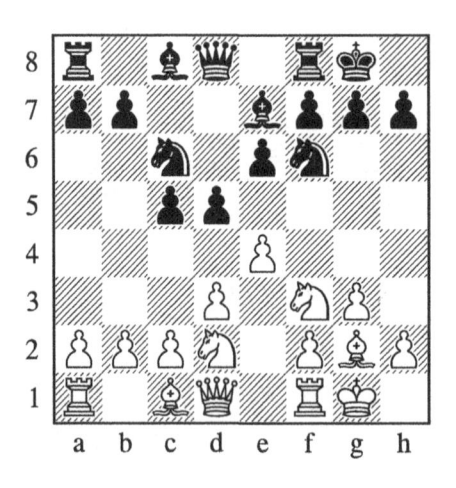

8. e5 ♘d7 9. ♖e1 b5 10. ♘f1 b4 11. h4 a5 12. ♗f4 a4 13. a3 bxa3 14. bxa3 ♘a5 15. ♘e3 ♗a6 16. ♗h3 d4

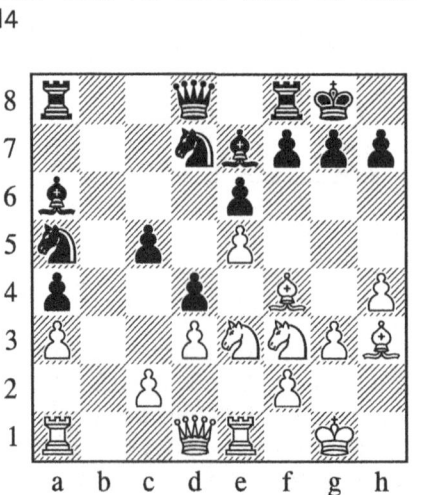

17. ♘f1 ♘b6 18. ♘g5 ♘d5 19. ♗d2 ♗xg5 20. ♗xg5 ♕d7 21. ♕h5 ♖fc8 22. ♘d2 ♘c3 23. ♗f6 ♕e8 24. ♘e4 g6??

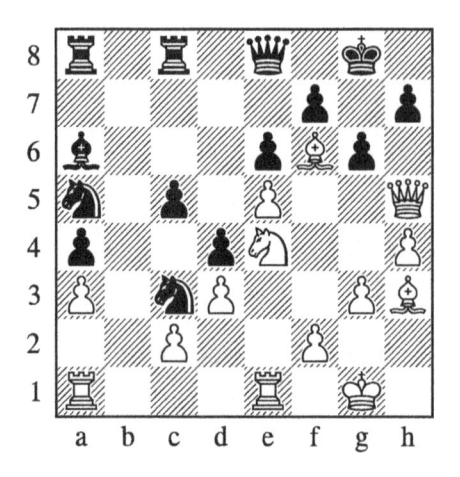

25. ♕g5 ♘xe4 26. ♖xe4 c4 27. h5 cxd3 28. ♖h4 ♖a7 29. ♗g2 dxc2?? 30. ♕h6 ♕f8 31. ♕xh7+ 1-0

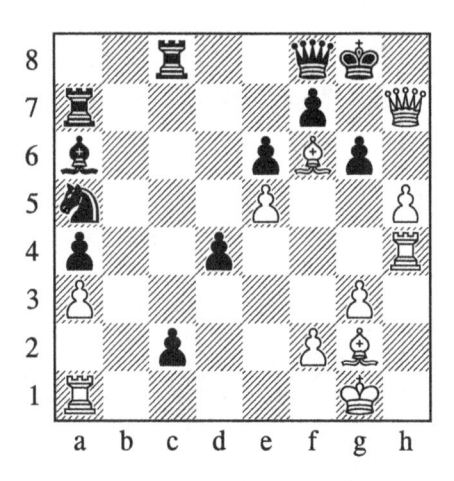

King's Indian Attack

Find the best move for White

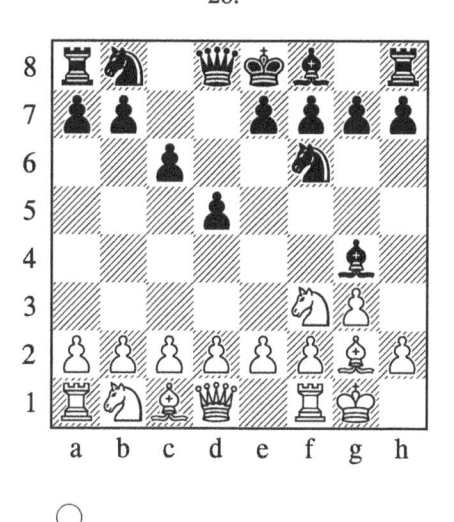

25.

26.

27.

28.

French Defense

History

The **French Defence** is a popular chess opening that has been played for hundreds of years. It gets its name from the fact that it was first documented in a game played by French chess players Philidor and de Kermur in the late 18th century. Over the years, the French Defense has been analyzed and refined by many great chess players, including Steinitz, Alekhine, and Fischer.

Basic ideas

The basic idea of the French Defense for White is to **control the center** of the board and **put pressure on Black's position**. To do this, White usually plays the pawn to e5, which aims to control the squares in the center of the board and open up lines for their pieces. One key idea is to take advantage of the **weaknesses in Black's pawn structure**, particularly the pawn on d5. Overall, as the White player, it is important to be **patient** and **play strategically** when facing the French Defense.

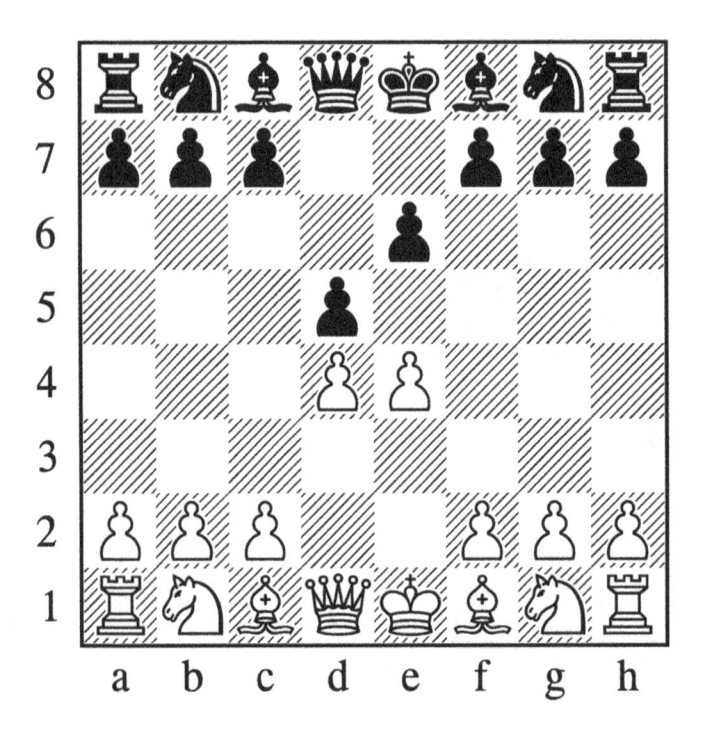

1. e4 e6 2. d4 d5

Top variations

Advance Variation: 3. e5

White gains some space advantage immediately, and prevents Black from developing their king's knight to its most natural square f6. Play usually continues with 3...c5 4. c3 ♘c6 5. ♘f3

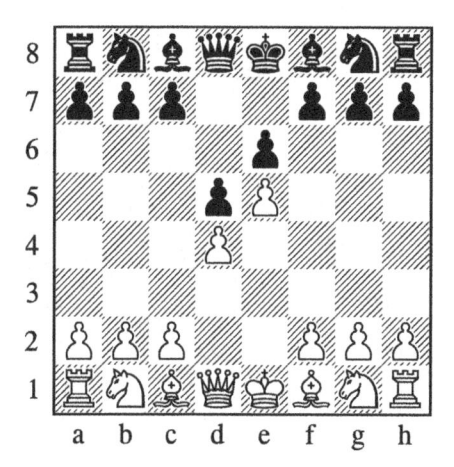

Exchange Variation: 3. exd5

Many White players find that the French Defence is very difficult opening for them to play against due to the closed structure. Thus, they choose to play the Exchange so that the position becomes simpler. White next plays 4. ♗d3, 4. ♘f3 or 4. ♗e3.

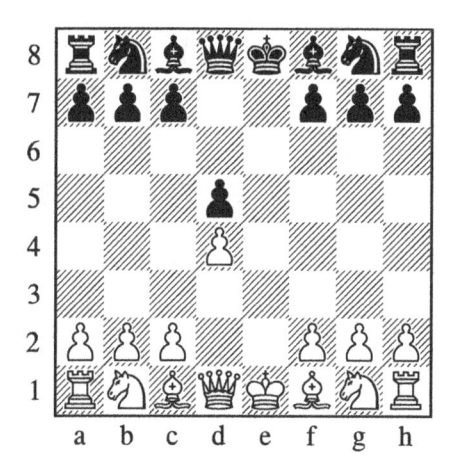

Main line

Classical Variation: 3. ♘c3

1. e4 e6 2. d4 d5 3. ♘c3 ♘f6 4. ♗g5

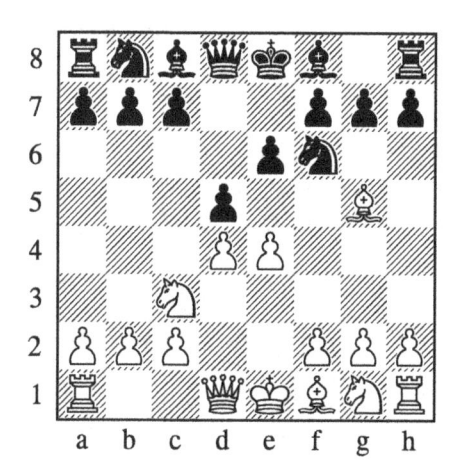

Where to put pawns and pieces

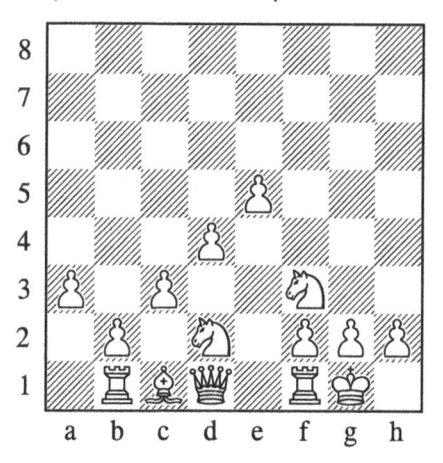

Did you know?

"The French bishop" on c8 is often referred to as "bad" or "poor" because it is blocked in by its own pawns and cannot immediately participate in the game.

French Defense

Model game

Boris Spassky vs Viktor Korchnoi
St. Peterburg (1999)

1. e4 e6 2. d4 d5 3. e5 c5 4. c3 ♞c6 5. ♘f3 ♛b6 6. a3 a5 7. ♗d3 ♝d7 8. ♗c2 h5 9. O-O ♞h6

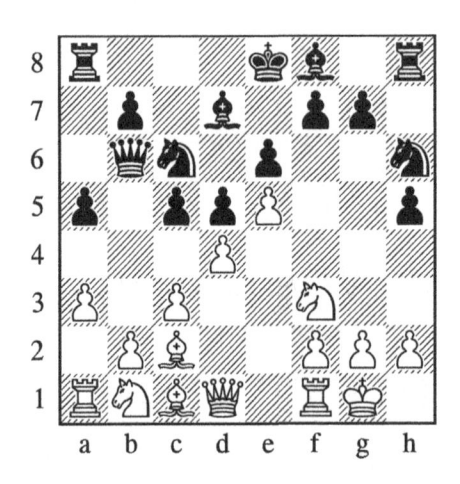

10. b3 ♝e7 11. ♖a2 cxd4 12. cxd4 ♖c8 13. ♗xh6 ♖xh6 14. ♕d2 ♖h8 15. h4 ♚f8 16. ♕f4 ♚g8 17. ♘bd2 g6 18. ♖d1 ♚g7 19. ♘f1 ♞a7 20. ♘g5 ♝e8

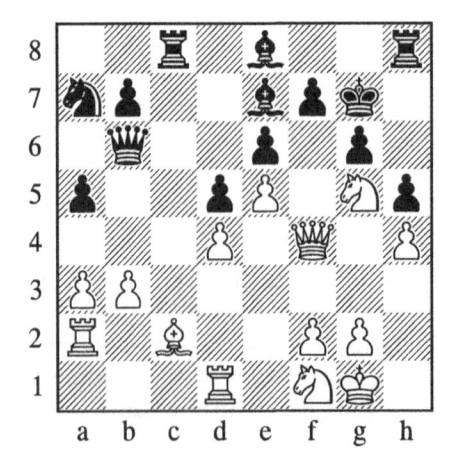

21. ♖d3 ♞b5 22. ♗d1 ♖c3 23. ♖ad2 ♕c7 24. a4 ♖xd3 25. ♖xd3 ♞c3 26. ♘g3 ♞xd1 27. ♖xd1 ♕b6

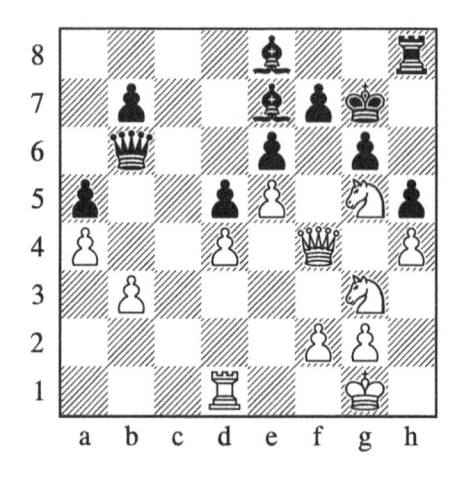

28. ♖d3 ♕c7 29. ♖f3 ♝d8 30. ♘e2 ♕e7 31. Qc1 ♕b4 32. ♘f4 ♝xg5 33. hxg5 ♝c6 34. ♕e3 ♖c8 35. ♚h2 ♝e8 36. ♘d3 ♕xb3 37. ♕f4 ♕xa4?? 38. ♕f6+ ♚g8 39. ♘f4 ♚h7? 40. ♘xe6 1-0

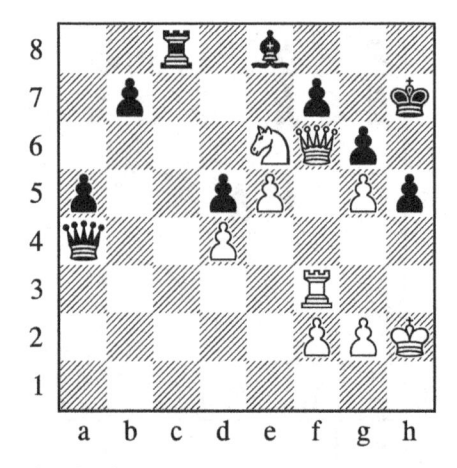

Chess Openings for Kids with White

French Defense

Find the best move for White

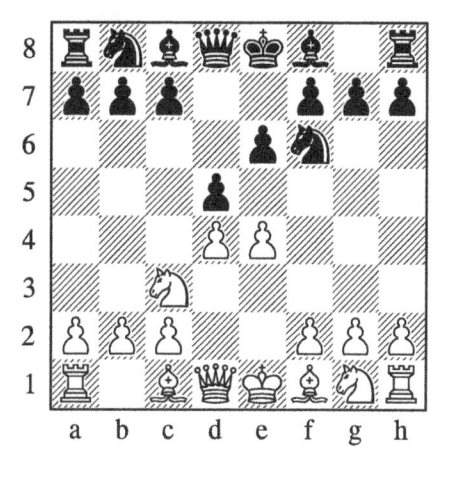

29.

○ _____

30.

○ _____

31.

○ _____

32.

○ _____

Caro-Kann Defense

History

The **Caro-Kann Defense** is named after two players who never actually played it together: Horatio Caro and Marcus Kann. Caro was a German chess player, while Kann was an Austrian journalist and chess enthusiast. The opening was named after them in the early 20th century, as they were both known for advocating its use.

Basic ideas

The Caro-Kann Defense is one of the most solid and defensive openings in chess, and is known for being difficult for White to crack. White should aim to **control the center** with your pawns and pieces, such as by playing pawn to e5. This will make it harder for Black to maneuver their pieces effectively. **Knights are particularly effective** in the Caro-Kann Defense, as they can jump over Black's pawns and put pressure on key squares. Be **patient** and look for opportunities to **build up** your position and **put pressure on Black** over time.

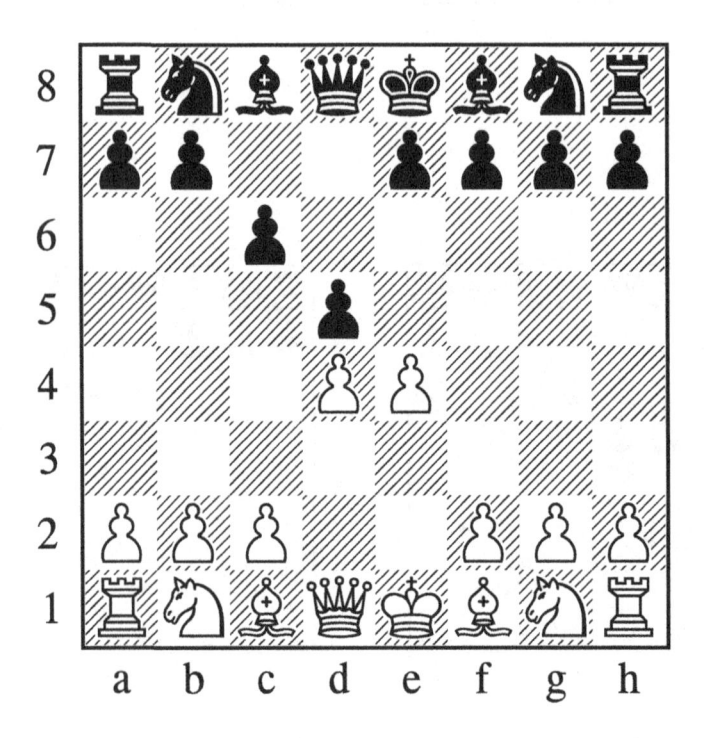

1. e4 c6 2. d4 d5

Top variations

Advance Variation: 3. e5

The Advance Variation was widely regarded as inferior for many years, but has since been revitalized. Black almost always plays 3...♗f5 to free the light-squared bishop outside the pawn chain.

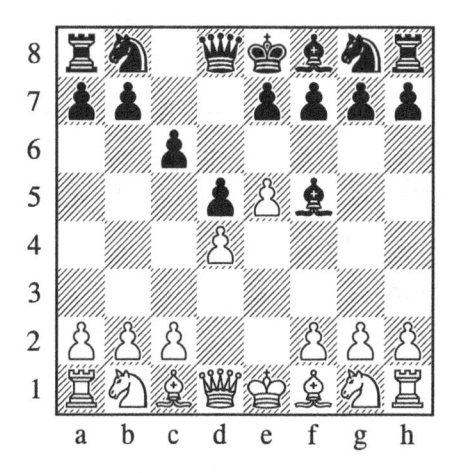

Exchange Variation: 3. exd5 cxd5

White exchanges on d5, and Black almost always responds with cxd5. This forms opposite-wing pawn majorities. Play usually continues with 4. ♗d3 ♘c6 5. c3

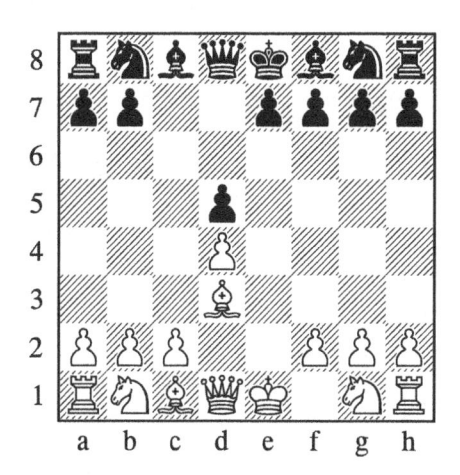

Main line

Classical Variation: 3. ♘c3

1. e4 c6 2. d4 d5 3. ♘c3 dxe4 4. ♘xe4 ♗f5 5. ♘g3 ♗g6

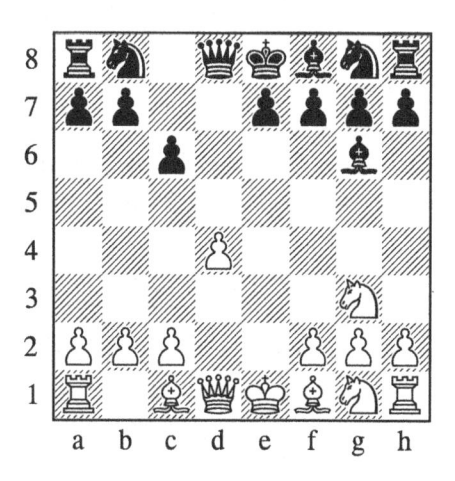

Where to put pawns and pieces

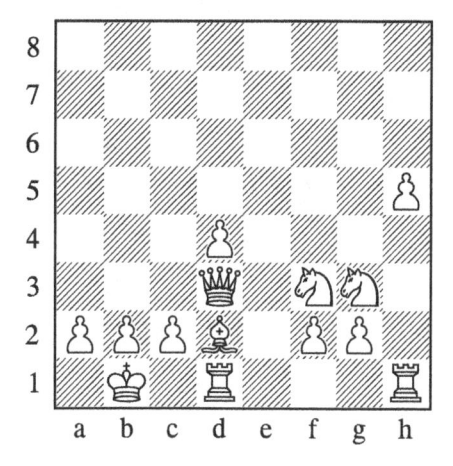

Did you know?

Caro-Kann Defense is sometimes jokingly called "Cockroach" (the Russian for cockroach is tarakan)

Chess Openings for Kids with White

Caro-Kann Defense

Model game

Magnus Carlsen vs Aleksandr Shimanov
Moscow (2019)

1. e4 c6 2. d4 d5 3. exd5 cxd5 4. ♗d3 ♘c6 5. c3 ♕c7 6. h3 ♘f6 7. ♘f3 e6 8. O-O ♗d6 9. ♖e1 b6 10. ♘bd2 ♗b7 11. ♕e2 O-O

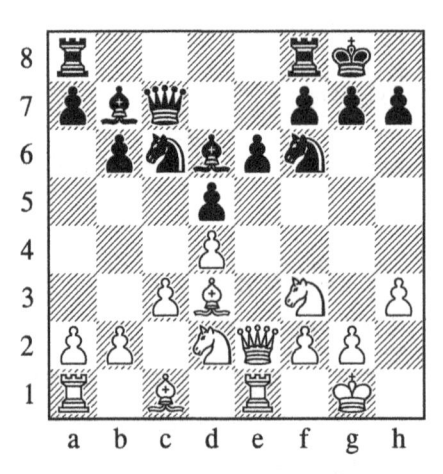

12. ♘e5 ♖ae8 13. ♗b1 ♘d7 14. ♘df3 f6 15. ♕d3 f5 16. ♗f4 ♘f6 17. ♗h2 ♘d8 18. a4 a5 19. ♕e2 ♘e4 20. ♗d3 f4 21. c4 ♖e7

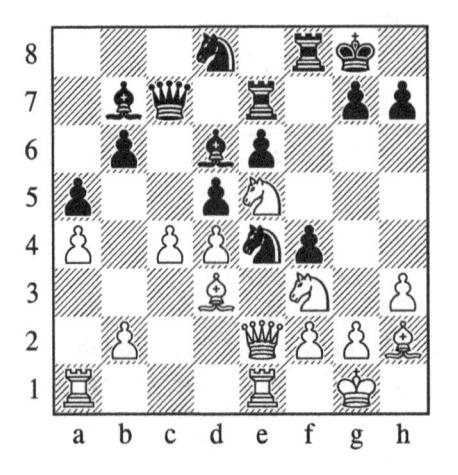

22. ♖ac1 ♕b8 23. cxd5 exd5 24. ♗b5 ♖xe5 25. ♘xe5 ♕d6 26. f3 ♘g3 27. ♗xg3 fxg3 28. ♕e3 ♘e6??

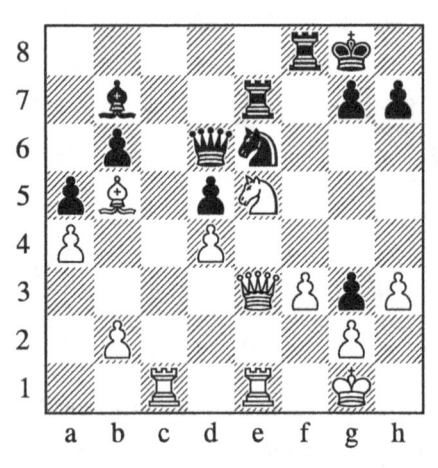

29. ♘c6 ♖ee8 30. ♕e5 ♕xe5 31. ♖xe5 ♔h8?! 32. ♘xa5 bxa5 33. ♗xe8 ♖xe8 34. ♖ce1 ♗c8 35. ♖xd5 ♖f8? 36. ♖xa5 ♘xd4 37. ♖a8 ♔g8 38. b4 ♖d8? 39. b5 ♔f7 40. b6 ♘c2?? 41. b7 ♘xe1 1-0

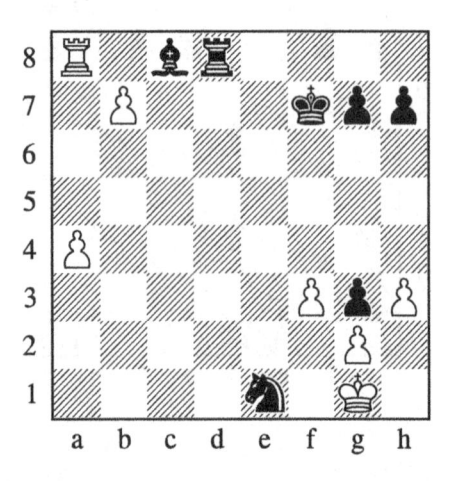

36 *Chess Openings for Kids with White*

Caro-Kann Defense

Find the best move for White

33.

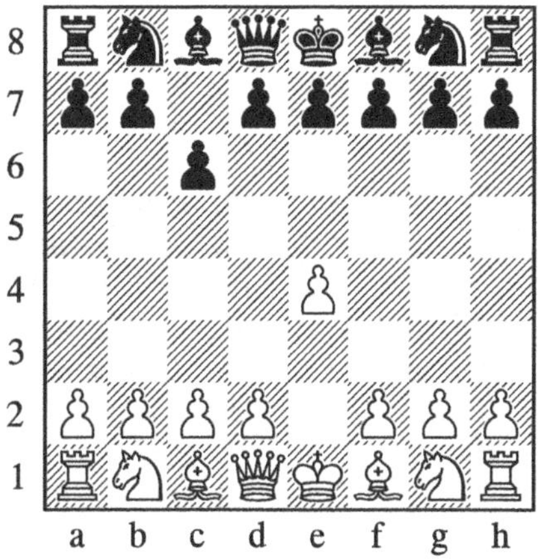

○ _____

34.

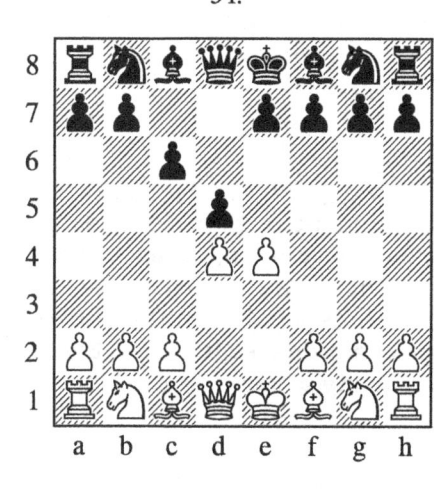

○ _____

35.

○ _____

36.

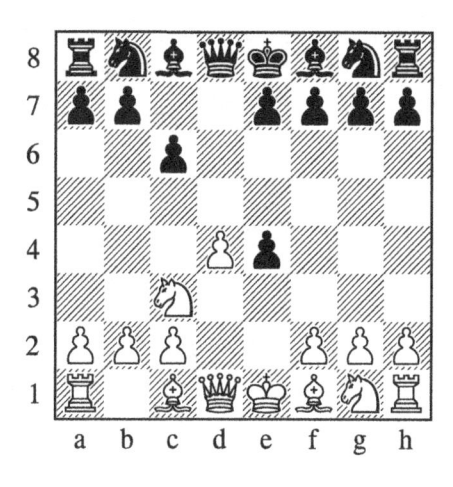

○ _____

London System

History

In the early years, the **London System** was popularized by James Mason, an Irish-born chess player, who played it several times during the 1880s. In 1922, large international chess tournament was organized in London. The opening which was previously named "Mason Variation" was quite popular in the tournament and as a result, became known as the "London System."

Basic ideas

The two greatest advantages of the London System are that it reduces the amount of time needed to study the opening and **it can be used against any set-up Black chooses**. London System allows for a **flexible position** – White can choose to push their pawns forward or exchange pieces, depending on the situation on the board. It can lead to **tactical opportunities**, especially if Black tries to attack the white position. Usually White attacks on the kingside with pieces.

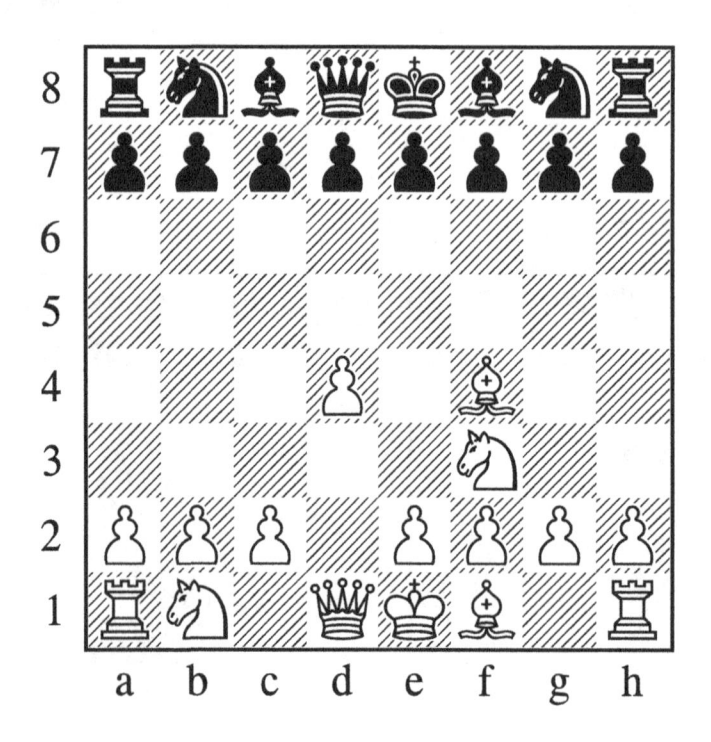

The London System setup

Top variations

The Modern London

Instead of developing 2. ♘f3, White can immediately play 2. ♗f4. Much like the Bishop's opening, White develops the bishop before the knight, ignoring the opening principle of "knights before bishops".

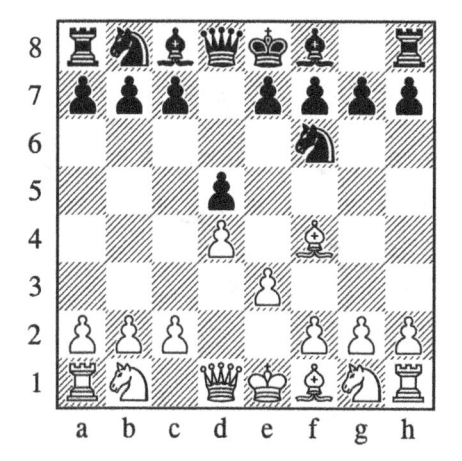

Rapport–Jobava System

Named after grandmasters Richárd Rapport and Baadur Jobava, this system can be a surprise against Black. Move order usually is 1. d4 d5 2. ♘c3 ♞f6 3. ♗f4. White can castle queenside and attack.

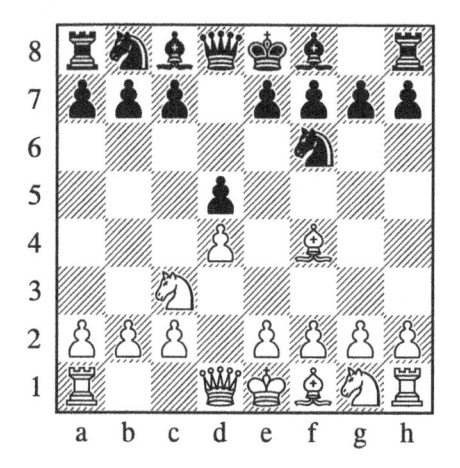

Main line

Classical line

1. d4 ♞f6 2. ♘f3 d5 3. ♗f4

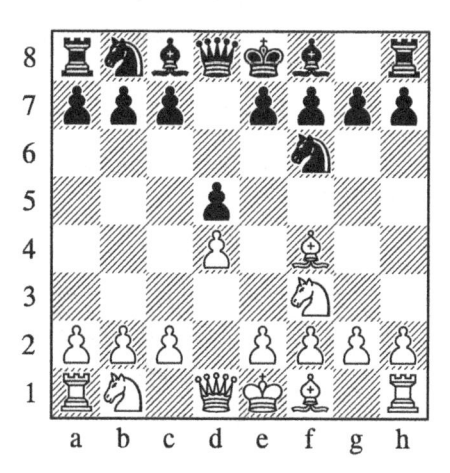

Where to put pawns and pieces

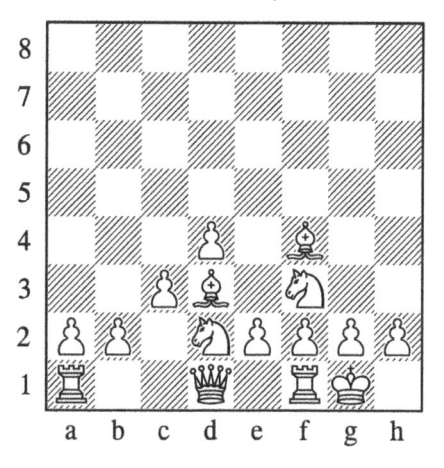

Did you know?
London system has been occasionally played by Super-Grandmasters Magnus Carlsen, Levon Aronian and Wei Yi.

Chess Openings for Kids with White

London System

Model game

Susan Polgar vs Peter Schaffarth
San Bernardino (1987)

1. d4 ♘f6 2. ♘f3 e6 3. ♗f4 c5 4. e3 d5 5. c3 ♗e7

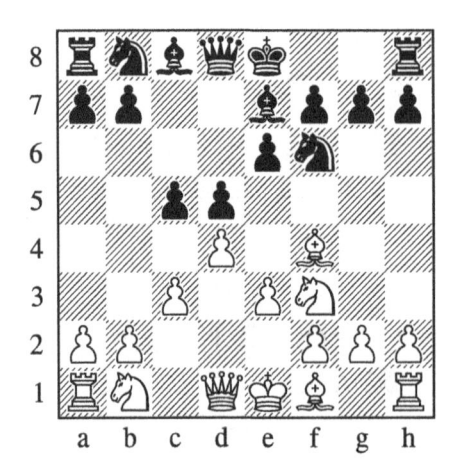

6. ♘bd2 O-O 7. ♗d3 b6 8. ♘e5 ♗b7 9. Qf3 ♘bd7

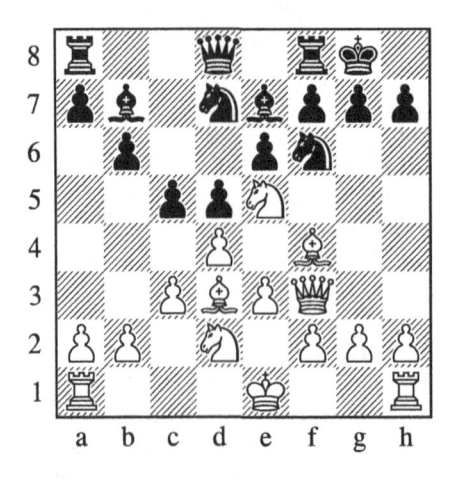

10. ♕h3 ♖e8 11. ♖d1?! c4?! 12. ♗c2 b5?! 13. ♘df3 g6??

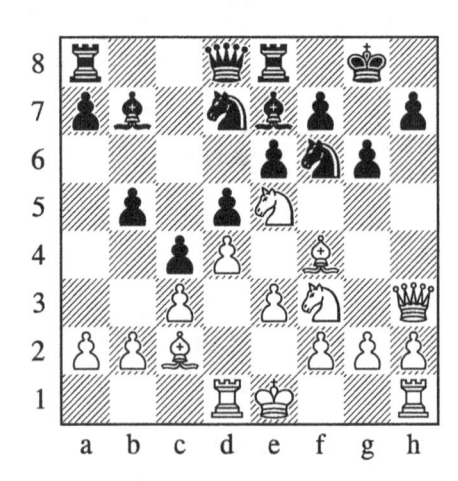

14. ♘xf7 ♕b6 15. ♗xg6 ♖f8 16. ♘3g5 1-0

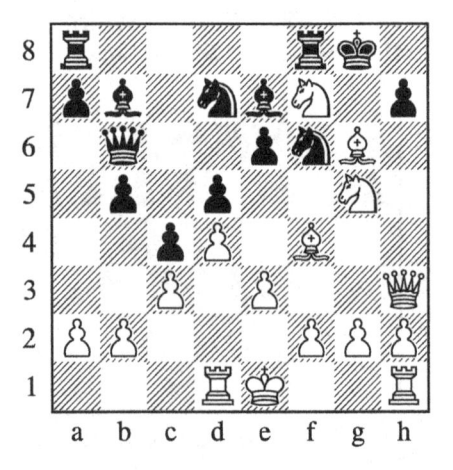

London System

Find the best move for White

37.

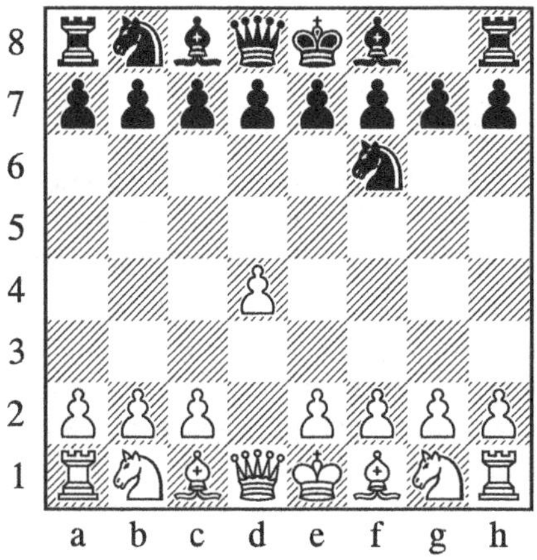

38.

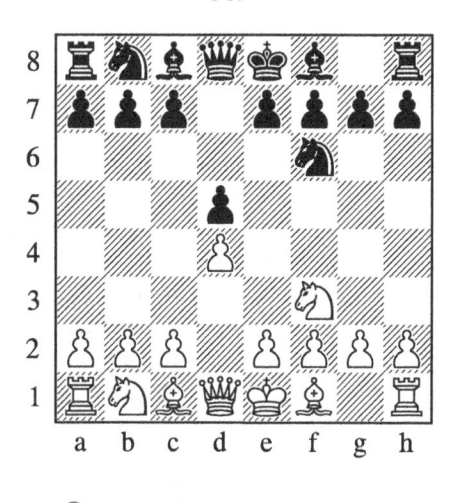

39.

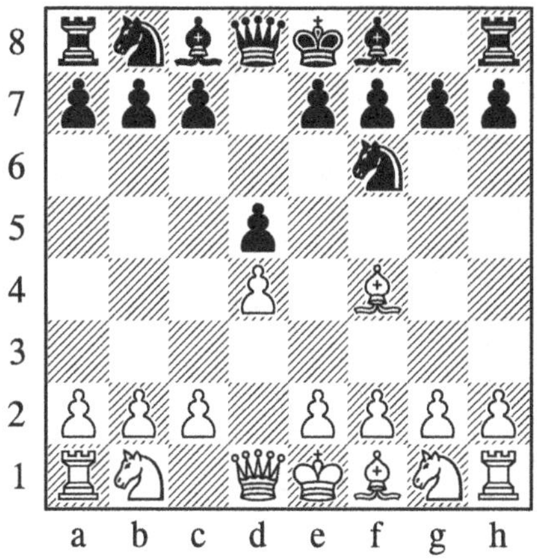

40.

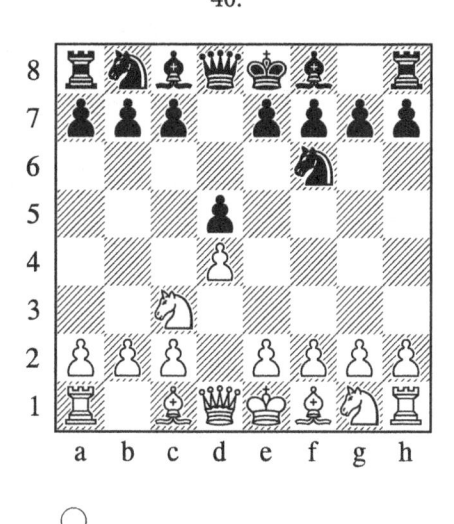

○ _____

○ _____

○ _____

○ _____

Colle System

History

The **Colle System** is a chess opening that was developed in the early 20th century by Belgian master Edgard Colle and further developed by George Koltanowski. It is a solid and reliable opening that can be used by white players to gain control of the center of the board and put pressure on their opponent.

Basic ideas

The basic idea of the Colle System is to set up a pawn structure that is similar to the London System. White moves their pawns to d4 and e3, and brings out their **knights and bishops to control the center** of the board. The difference with the Colle System is that white bring the bishop to d3 instead of f4. The Colle System is a good opening for players who prefer a **more defensive style of play**. It can be difficult for black to launch an attack against white's position, and white can **gradually build up their position** and **prepare for an attack** of their own.

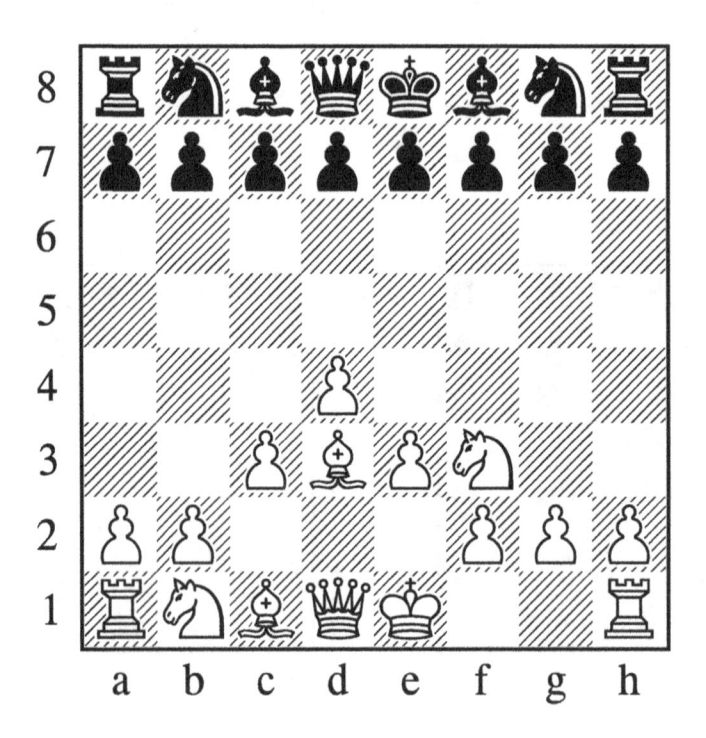

The Colle System setup

Top variations

Colle–Zukertort System

One variation of the Colle is the Colle–Zukertort System (named after Johannes Zukertort), characterized by developing the dark-squared bishop on b2.

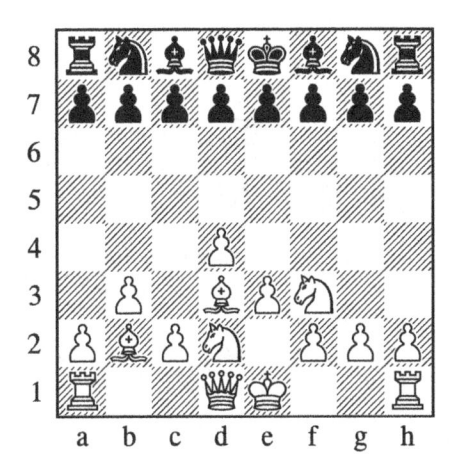

The typical plan is: 1. d4 d5 2. ♘f3 e6 3. e3 ♞f6 4. ♗d3 c5 5. b3 ♞c6 6. 0-0 ♗d6 7. ♗b2 0-0. White will eventually put the knight on e5, play moves f4, ♖f3-♖h3, try to open up the dark-squared bishop and go for a kingside attack.

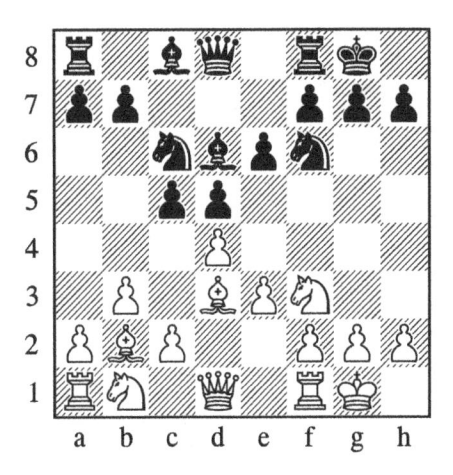

Main line

1. d4 d5 2. ♘f3 ♞f6 3. e3 c5 4. c3 e6 5. ♗d3

Where to put pawns and pieces

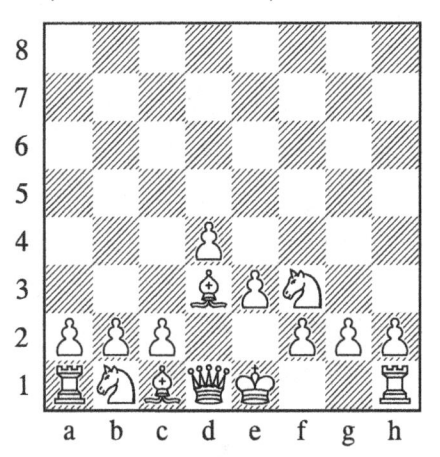

Did you know?

The Colle system has been frequently played at grandmaster level by Artur Yusupov and Susan Polgar.

Chess Openings for Kids with White

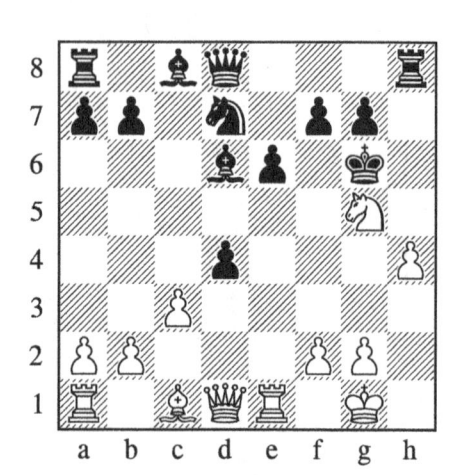

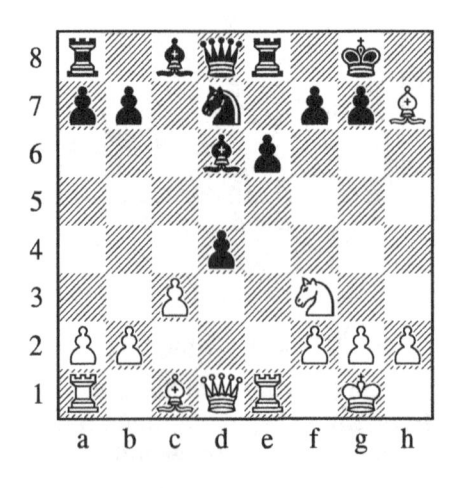

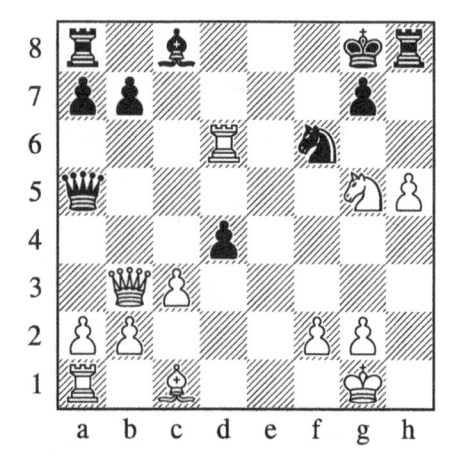

Colle System

Model game

Edgar Colle vs John James O'Hanlon
Nice (1930)

1. d4 d5 2. ♘f3 ♞f6 3. e3 c5 4. c3 e6 5. ♗d3 ♝d6 6. ♘bd2 ♞bd7

7. 0-0 0-0 8. ♖e1 ♜e8 9. e4 dxe4 10. ♘xe4 ♞xe4 11. ♗xe4 cxd4 12. ♗xh7+?!

12...♚xh7 13. ♘g5+ ♚g6?? 14. h4 ♜h8??

15. ♖xe6+ ♞f6 16. h5+ ♚h6 17. ♖xd6 ♛a5 18. ♘xf7+ ♚h7 19. ♘g5+ ♚g8?! 20. ♕b3+ 1–0

44 Chess Openings for Kids with White

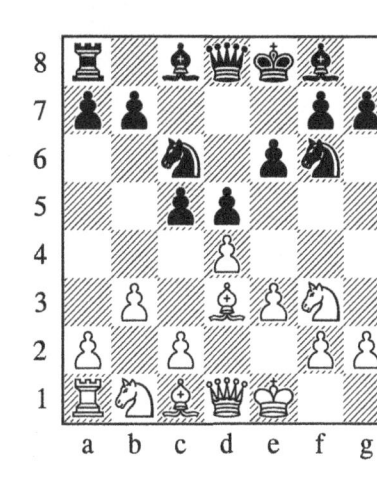

Colle System

Find the best move for White

41.

○ _____

42.

○ _____

43.

○ _____

44.

○ _____

Scotch Game

History

The **Scotch game** is a chess opening that got its name from a match played by mail in 1824 between Edinburgh and London. It was really popular in the 19th century, but by 1900, top players lost interest in it because it gave Black an easy way to catch up. In more recent times, the Scotch game has become popular again, as famous chess players Garry Kasparov and Jan Timman started using it to surprise their opponents and avoid the Ruy Lopez, which was very well-known and often played.

Basic ideas

The Scotch game is a **very aggressive opening** and can lead to some exciting games! It's important to remember to **control the center** of the board and **develop your pieces quickly** to put pressure on your opponent. White has natural easy development with an open file, but so does Black. This makes the opening **ideal for beginners**, as development is natural for both sides, and it is **very low in theory**.

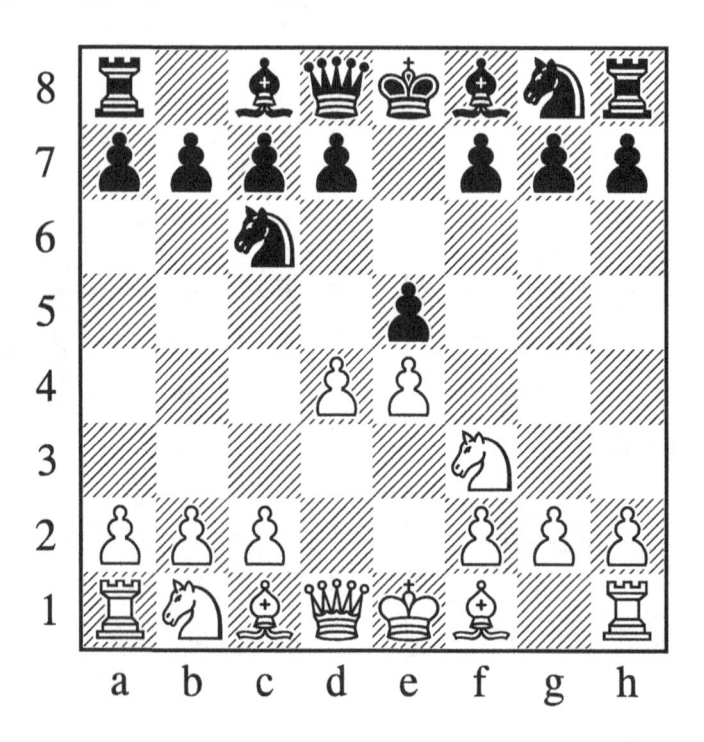

1. e4 e5 2. ♘f3 ♞c6 3. d4

Top variations

Scotch Gambit: 4. Bc4

After 4...Bc5 and 5. c3 Black can accept the gambit with 5...dxc3, but it is risky because White will gain a lead in development after 6. Bxf7+ Kxf7 7. Qd5+ and Qxc5.

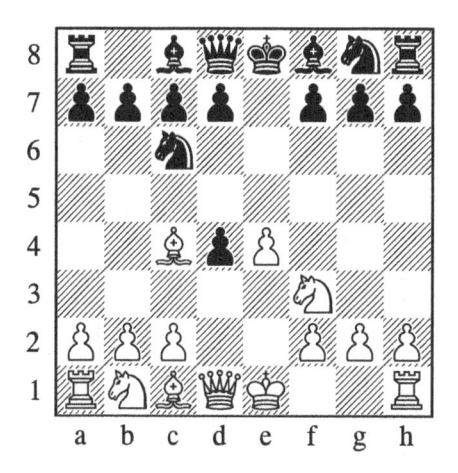

Göring Gambit: 4. c3

White sacrifices one or two pawns in return for a lead in development, and typically follows up by putting pressure on f7 with Bc4, Qb3 and sometimes Ng5, while Nc3–d5 is another common motif.

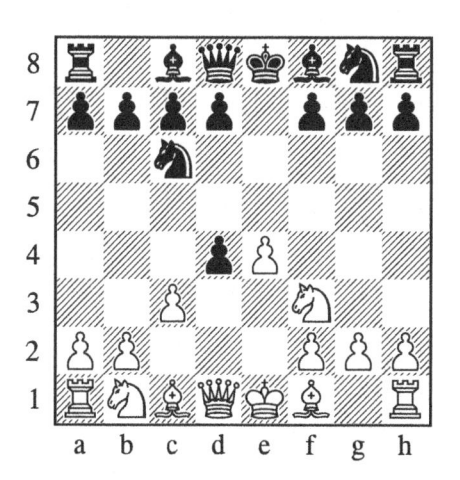

Main line

Classical Variation: 4...Bc5

1. e4 e5 2. ♘f3 ♞c6 3. d4 exd4 4. ♘xd4 ♝c5 5. ♗e3

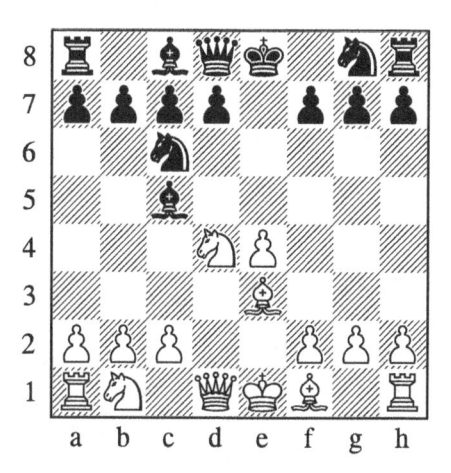

Where to put pawns and pieces

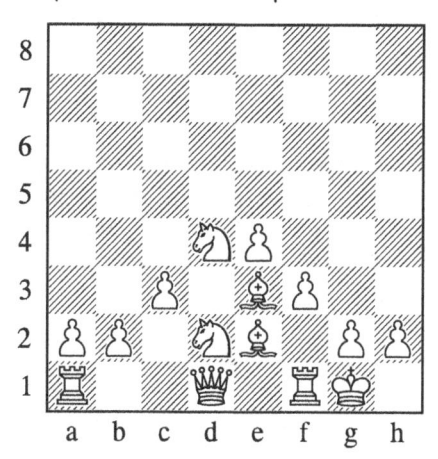

Did you know?

The Scotch Game is the third most popular opening arising from the King's knight game (1. e4 e5 2. ♘f3 ♞c6) after the Ruy Lopez and the Italian Game.

Chess Openings for Kids with White

Scotch Game

Model game

Garry Kasparov vs Anatoly Karpov
Tilburg (1991)

1. e4 e5 2. ♘f3 ♞c6 3. d4 exd4 4. ♘xd4 ♞f6 5. ♘xc6 bxc6 6. e5 ♛e7 7. ♕e2 ♞d5 8. c4 ♝a6 9. b3 g6 10. f4 f6 11. ♗a3 ♛f7

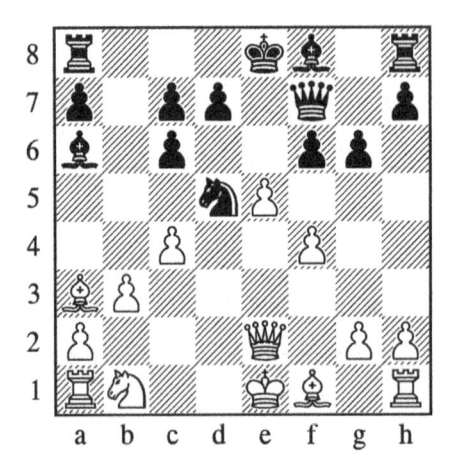

12. ♕d2 ♞b6 13. c5 ♝xf1 14. cxb6 axb6 15. e6 dxe6 16. ♗xf8 ♜d8 17. ♕b2 ♝xg2+ 18. ♕xg2 ♚xf8 19. ♕xc6 ♜d6 20. ♕c3 ♚g7 21. ♘d2 ♜hd8 22. 0-0-0 ♛e8?!

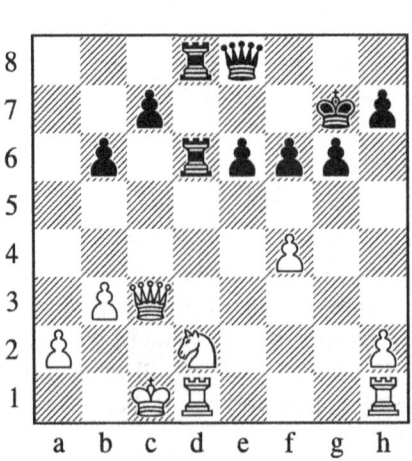

23. ♕xc7+ ♜8d7 24. ♕c2 ♛b8 25. ♘c4 ♜d5 26. ♕f2 ♛c7 27. ♕xb6 ♛xf4+ 28. ♕e3 ♛g4 29. ♜dg1 ♛h4 30. ♜g3 e5 31. ♜h3 ♛g4 32. ♜g1 ♜d1+ 33. ♜xd1 ♛xd1+

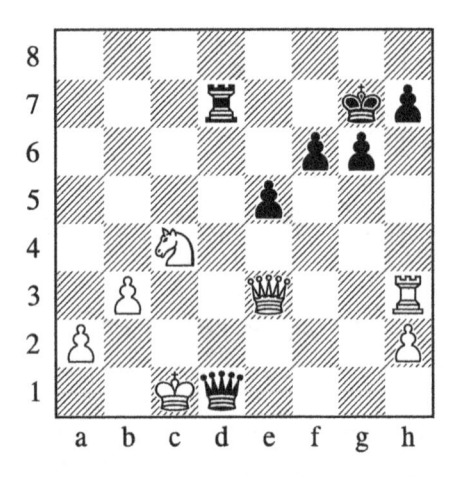

34. ♔b2 h5 35. ♜g3 ♛h1 36. ♕f2 h4 37. ♕g2 ♛xg2+ 38. ♜xg2 g5 39. a4 ♚g6 40. a5 e4 41. b4 h3 42. ♜g3 ♜h7 43. a6 f5 44. ♜a3 1-0

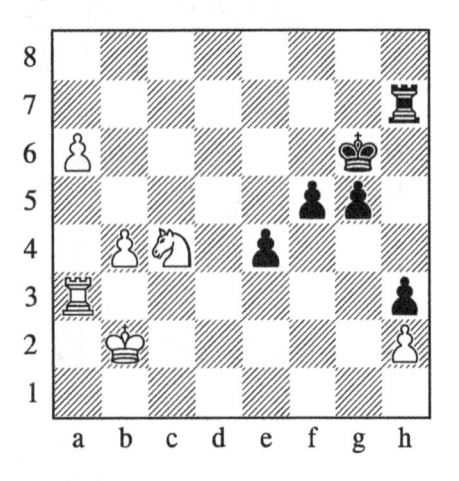

48 *Chess Openings for Kids with White*

Scotch Game

Find the best move for White

45.

46.

47.

48.

○ _____

○ _____

○ _____

○ _____

Vienna Game

History

The **Vienna Game** was originally called **Hamppe's Game** after Carl Hamppe (1815-1876) and took its current name in the 1890's due to its ongoing popularity in Vienna, for centuries the capital of the Holy Roman and Austro-Hungarian Empires. The opening is considered to be very aggressive and can lead to some exciting attacking play.

Basic ideas

Here are some basic ideas for playing the Vienna Game. **Control the center** – put pressure on d5 square with your pawn on e4, knight on c3 and your light-squared bishop. **Develop your minor pieces** to active squares. You can also consider pushing your d-pawn to **open up lines** for your queen and bishop. The Vienna Game is known for its aggressive play. Look for opportunities to **attack your opponent's pieces** and **put pressure** on their position. Make sure to **castle** your king to safety, either on the kingside or queenside, depending on the position.

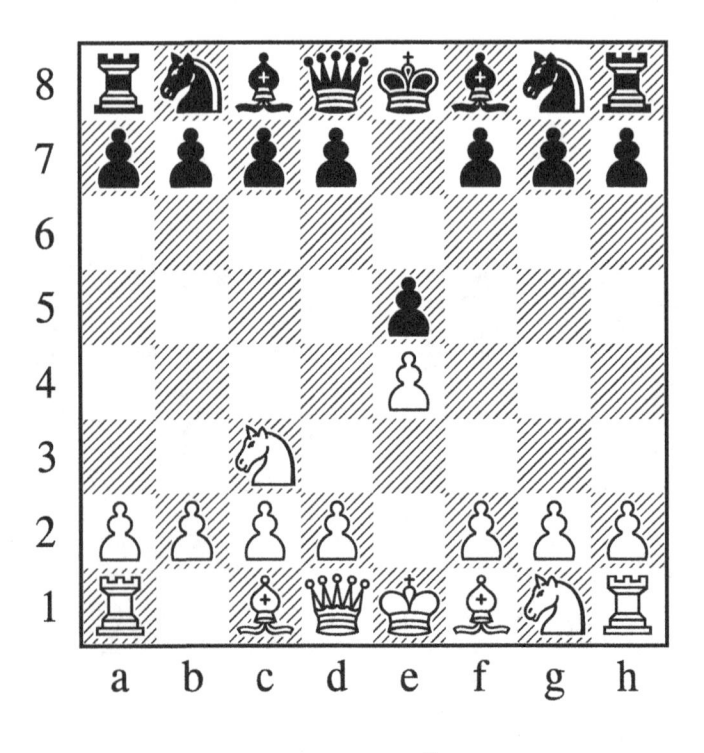

1. e4 e5 2. ♘c3

Chess Openings for Kids with White

Top variations

Vienna Gambit: 3. f4

At grandmaster level, the gambit move 3. f4 is considered too risky an opening. However, moves other than 3...d5 give White at least an edge, making this a good choice for aggressive play at lower levels.

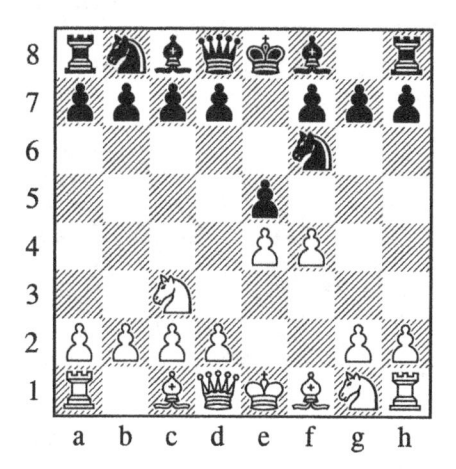

Max Lange Defence: 2...♞c6 3. ♗c4

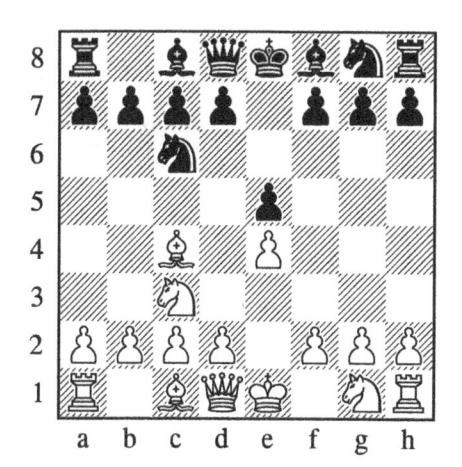

This sequence of opening moves is not an effective way for white to maintain any advantage, as pieces lack harmony. However, if Black plays copycat move 3...♗c5, after 4. ♕g4, white has upper hand.

Main line

Falkbeer Variation: 3. g3

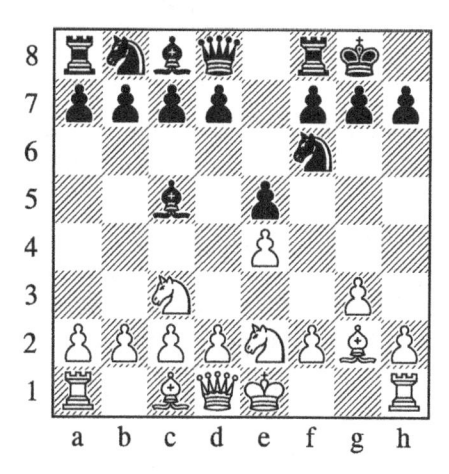

1. e4 e5 2. ♘c3 ♞f6 3. g3 ♗c5 4. ♗g2 O-O 5. ♘ge2

Where to put pawns and pieces

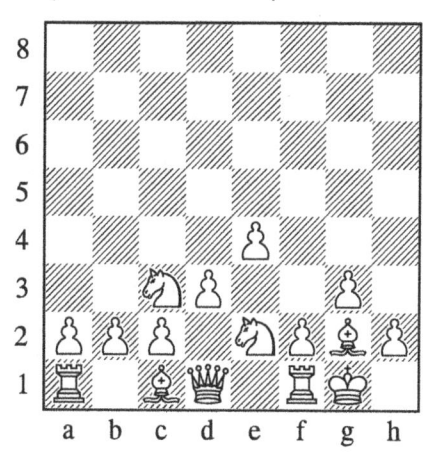

Did you know?

American chess master Weaver W. Adams once famously claimed that the Vienna Game led to a forced win for White.

Chess Openings for Kids with White

Vienna Game

Model game

Alexander Alekhine vs Richard Teichmann
Berlin (1921)

1. e4 e5 2. ♘c3 ♞c6 3. ♗c4 ♞f6
4. d3 ♝c5 5. f4 d6 6. ♘f3 ♝g4

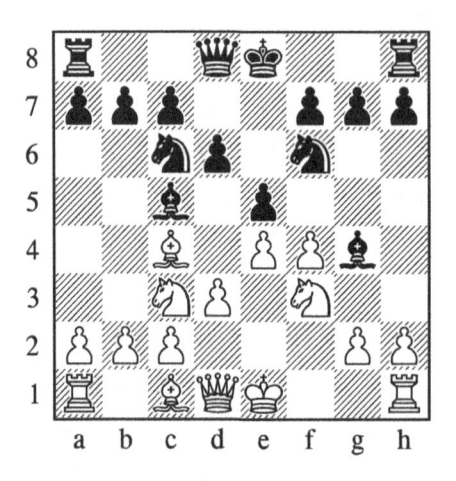

7. ♘a4 a6 8. ♘xc5 dxc5 9. O-O ♛e7 10. h3 ♝xf3 11. ♕xf3 O-O 12. ♗e3 exf4 13. ♕xf4 ♞e5 14. ♗b3 ♜ae8?!

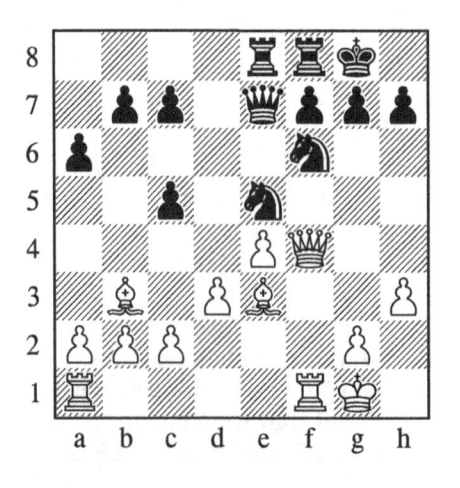

15. ♕f2 ♞fd7 16. ♖ad1 b6 17. c3?! ♞g6? 18. ♕f5 ♚h8 19. ♗f2 ♜d8 20. ♗g3 ♞de5 21. d4 cxd4 22. cxd4 ♞c6

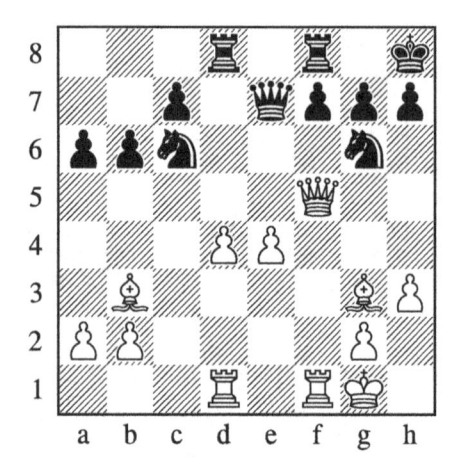

23. d5?! ♞ce5 24. h4 ♛c5+ 25. ♚h2 f6 26. ♖c1 ♛d6 27. ♖c6 ♛e7?! 28. ♖e6 ♛d7 29. h5 ♞e7 30. ♕h3 ♞f7 31. ♗f4 h6 1-0

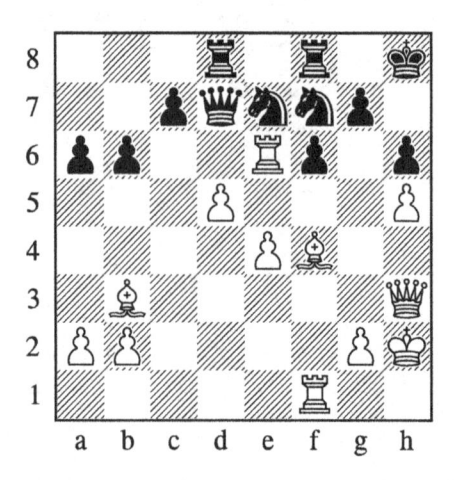

Vienna Game

Find the best move for White

49.

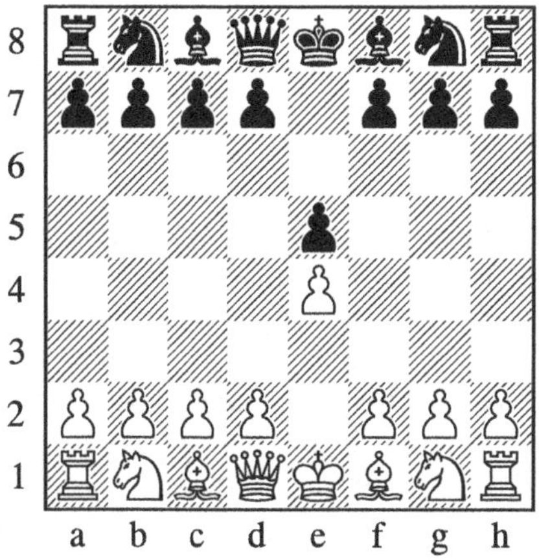

50.

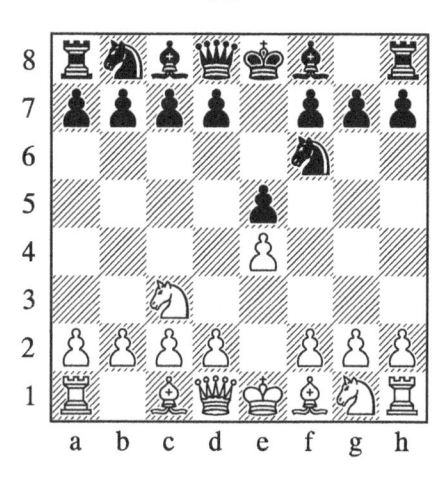

51.

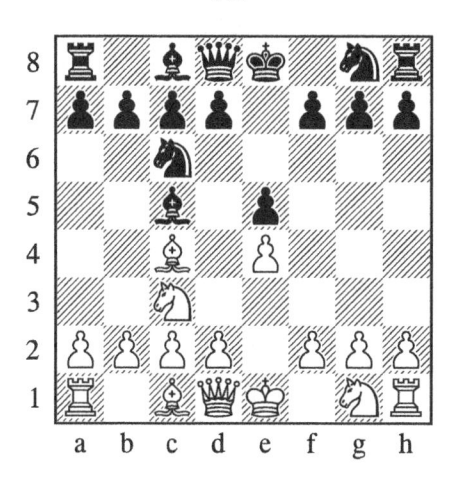

52.

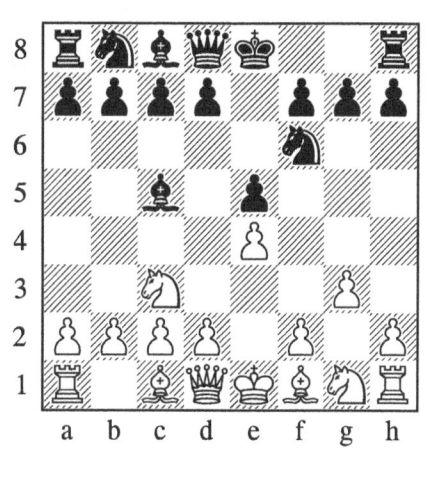

Scandinavian Defense

History

The **Scandinavian Defense** is one of the oldest recorded openings. It was mentioned in the 1497 Lucena's book "Repetition of Love and the Art of Playing Chess with 150 Games". It's named after the Scandinavian countries and is sometimes called the Center Counter Defense. Although opening has never enjoyed widespread popularity among top players, it has been occasionally played by likes Larsen, Anand and Carlsen.

Basic ideas

The Scandinavian Defense is a relatively **uncommon opening**. Black tries to break White's centre and stop white from taking control. White normally captures the pawn with 2. exd5 and Black usually recaptures with 2...♛xd5, bringing out his queen and providing White with a target to attack. One general idea is to play pawn to d4 and put your knight on the excellent e5 square via f3. You should follow general opening principles – **quickly develop** your pieces, **control the center** and **castle**.

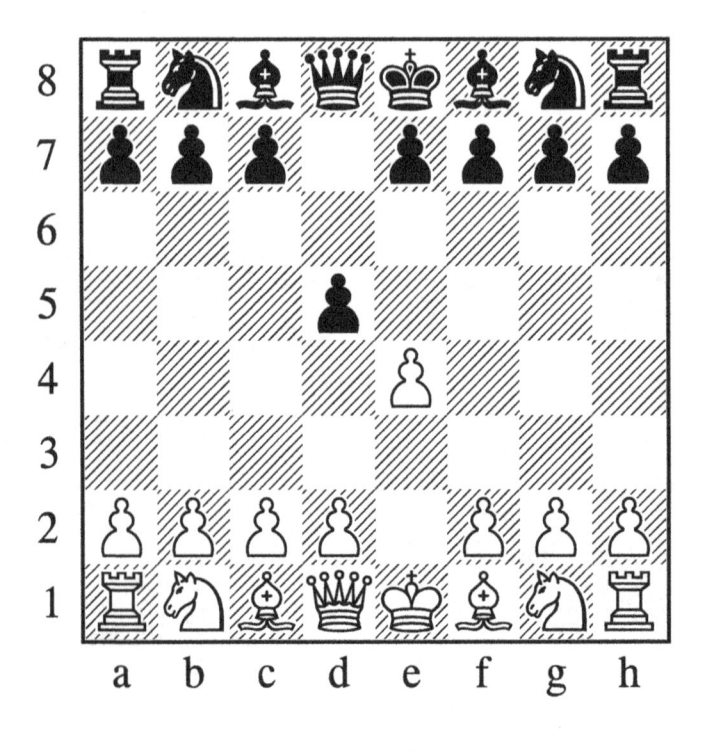

1. e4 d5

Top variations

Modern Variation: 2...♞f6 3. d4

The Blacks idea is to delay capturing the d5-pawn for another move, avoiding the loss of time that Black suffers in the ...♛xd5 lines after 3. ♞c3. Play continues with 3...♞xd5 4. ♞f3.

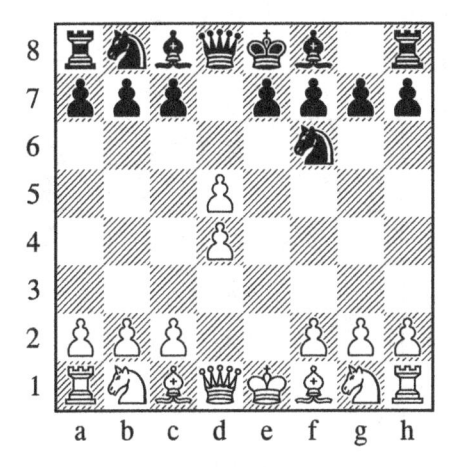

Valencian Variation: 3...♛d8

The retreat with 3...♛d8 may be the oldest of all Scandinavian lines. Prior to the 20th century, it was often considered the main line, but is somewhat passive. You can play 4. d4 ♞f6 5. ♞f3 here.

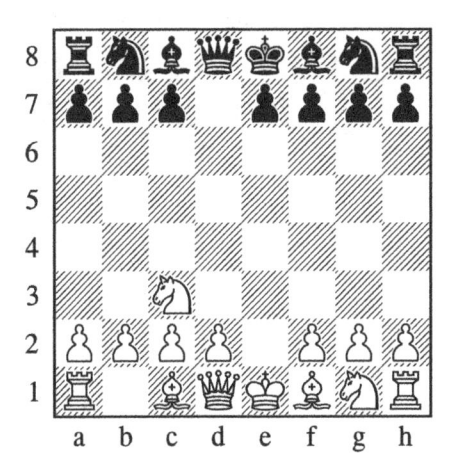

Main line

Classical Variation

1. e4 d5 2. exd5 ♛xd5 3. ♞c3 ♛a5 4. d4 ♞f6 5. ♞f3 c6 6. ♗c4

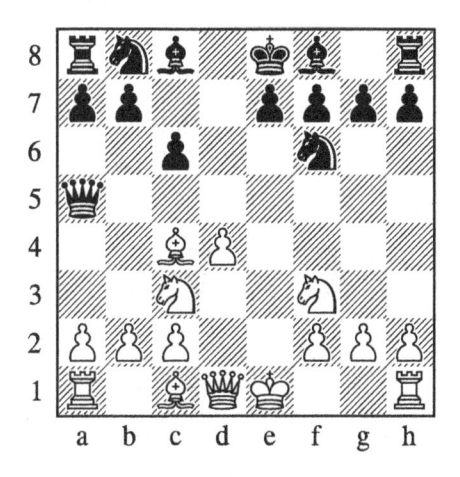

Where to put pawns and pieces

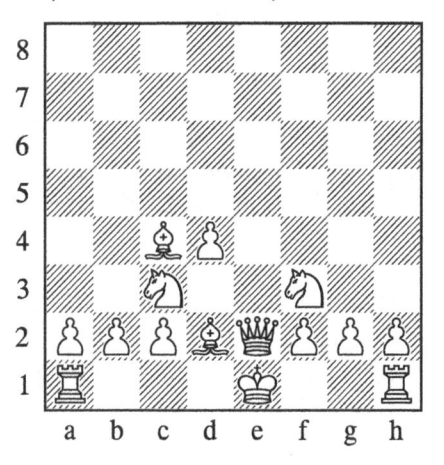

Did you know?

Scandinavian opening game, played in Valencia around 1475, may be the first recorded game of modern chess.

Chess Openings for Kids with White

Scandinavian Defense

Model game

Viswanathan Anand vs Joel Lautier
Biel (1997)

1. e4 d5 2. exd5 ♕xd5 3. ♘c3 ♕a5 4. d4 ♘f6 5. ♘f3 c6 6. ♗c4 ♗f5 7. ♘e5 e6

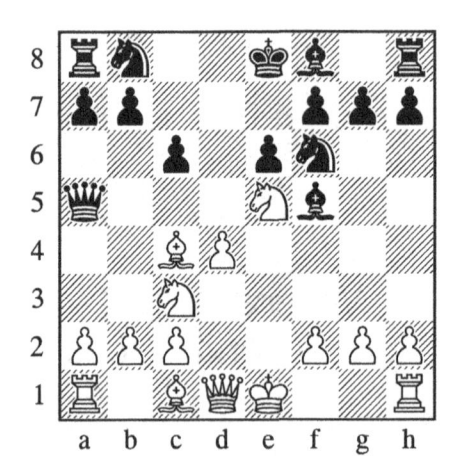

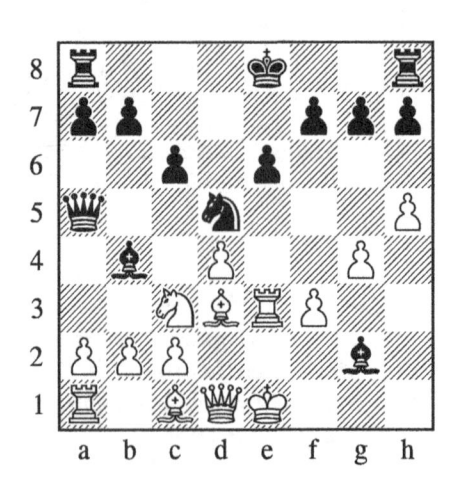

16. ♔f2 ♗xc3 17. bxc3 ♕xc3 18. ♖b1 ♕xd4 19. ♖xb7 ♖d8 20. h6 gxh6?!

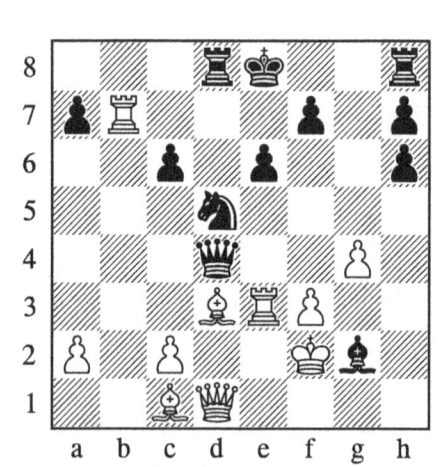

8. g4 ♗g6 9. h4 ♘bd7 10. ♘xd7 ♘xd7 11. h5 ♗e4 12. ♖h3 ♗g2 13. ♖e3 ♘b6 14. ♗d3 ♘d5 15. f3 ♗b4??

21. ♗g6 ♘e7 22. ♕xd4 ♖xd4 23. ♖d3 ♖d8 24. ♖xd8+ ♔xd8 25. ♗d3 1-0

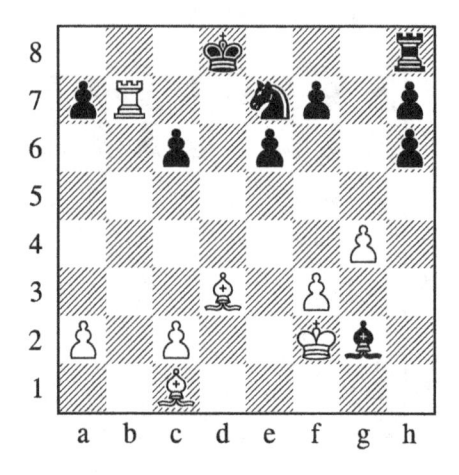

Scandinavian Defense

Find the best move for White

53.

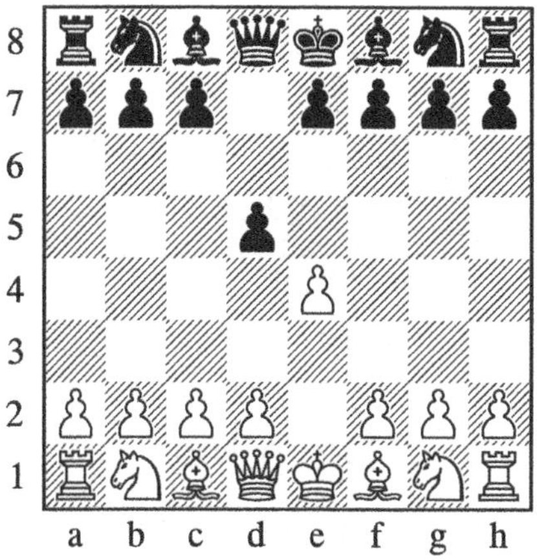

54.

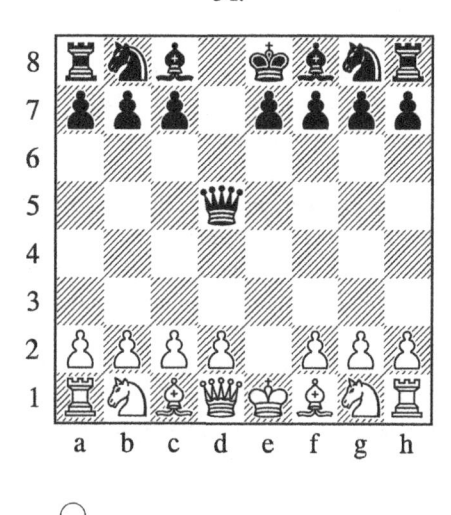

○ _____

○ _____

55.

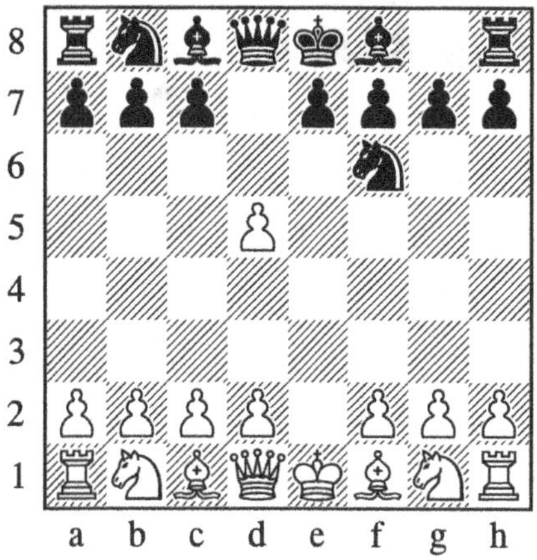

56.

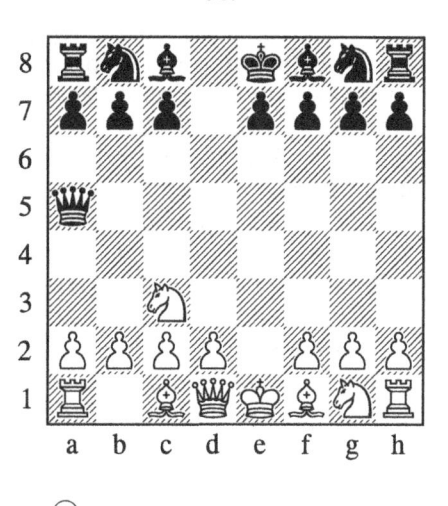

○ _____

○ _____

Bishop's Opening

History and Ideas

The **Bishop's Opening** is an ancient chess opening that dates from the 18th century to the days of Romantic chess. It was the favourite opening choice by François-André Danican Philidor. The Bishop's Opening used to be called "The Truth" back in the 19th century.

White **develops the light square bishop before bringing the knight** to f3. The main point is to develop the bishop to a good square while targeting the weak f7. By ignoring the beginner's rule "develop knights before bishops", **White leaves its f-pawn unblocked**, preserving the possibility of f2–f4.

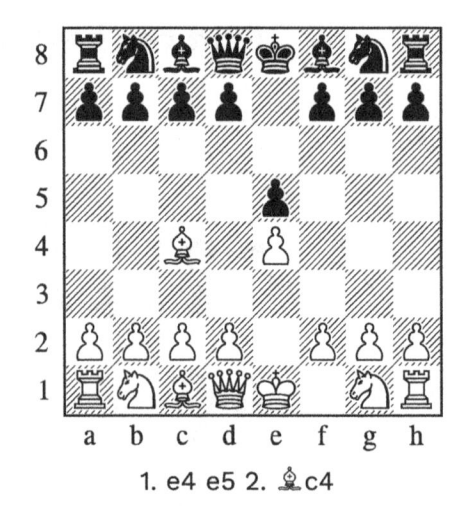

1. e4 e5 2. ♗c4

Main line

1. e4 e5 2. ♗c4 ♘f6 3. d3

Trompowsky Attack

History and Ideas

The opening is named after the one-time Brazilian champion Octávio Trompowsky (1897–1984) who played it in the 1930s and 1940s. Chess master Karel Opočenský (1892–1975) also played it in the 1930s, and the opening is also known as the Opočenský Opening.

The **Trompowsky Attack** is a new opening with less theory which involves White **immediately putting the bishop on g5 attacking the knight**. Usually in most variations (2...Ne4 or 2...e6) Black avoids doubled pawns, but sometimes accepts them.

1. d4 ♘f6 2. ♗g5

Main line

1. d4 ♘f6 2. ♗g5 ♘e4 3. ♗f4 c5 4. f3

Chess Openings for Kids with White

Alekhine's Defense

History and Ideas

Alekhine's Defense is a chess opening that was named after Alexander Alekhine, a former World Chess Champion. The opening was first introduced in the early 1920s and was popularized by Alekhine during his games.

The basic idea of Alekhine's Defense is for Black to allow White to **control the center with pawns**, and then launch a counterattack on White's center with minor pieces. The game immediately **loses any sense of symmetry** or balance, which makes the opening a good choice for aggressive fighting players.

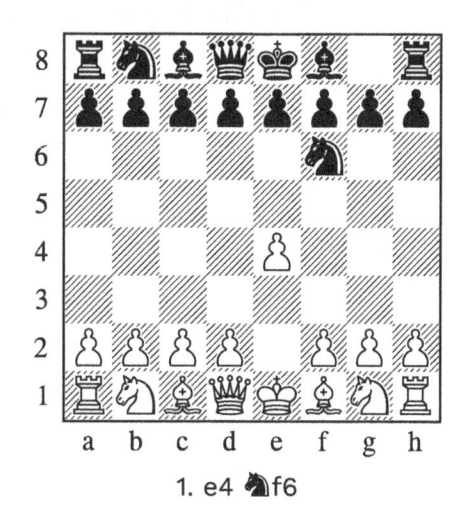

1. e4 ♞f6

Main line

1. e4 ♞f6 2. e5 ♞d5 3. d4 d6 4. ♘f3

Bird's Opening

History and Ideas

Bird's Opening is an aggressive and less common opening, named after the chess player Henry Bird. This opening weakens the h4-to-e1 diagonal, and weakens White's kingside, but helps control the centre and is good for players who don't want to study openings.

The main idea of the Bird's Opening is to **control the center** with the pawn on f4 and to prepare for a **quick development** of the kingside pieces. It often leads to **open and unbalanced positions** where both sides have many options and opportunities for tactics.

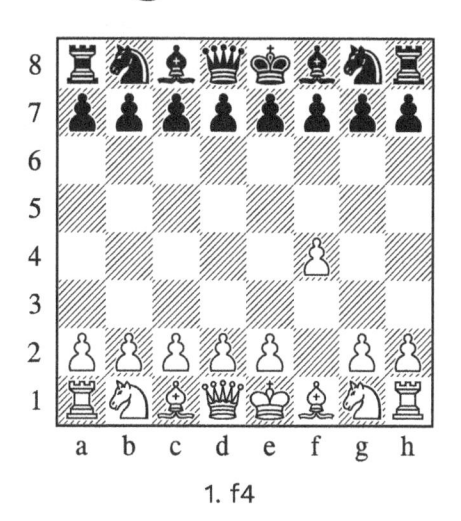

1. f4

Main line

1. f4 d5 2. ♘f3 g6 3. g3 ♗g7 4. ♗g2 ♞f6 5. O-O

Chess Openings for Kids with White

Solutions to Exercises

1) 2. ♘f3
2) 3. ♗b5
3) 4. ♗a4
4) 5. O-O
5) 2. ♘f3
6) 3. ♗c4
7) 4. c3
8) 5. d3 (or 5. d4)
9) 2. c4
10) 3. ♘f3
11) 2. ♘f3 (or 2. e3, or 2. e4)
12) 4. ♘c3
13) 2. ♘f3
14) 3. d4
15) 4. ♘xd4
16) 5. ♘c3
17) 2. ♘c3 (or 2. g3)
18) 2. ♘f3 (or 2. ♘c3)
19) 3. ♘f3
20) 4. g3
21) 2. c4
22) 3. e3
23) 3. e3
24) 4. ♘c3
25) 2. g3
26) 3. ♗g2
27) 4. O-O
28) 5. d3
29) 2. d4
30) 3. e5 (or 3. ♘c3)
31) 3. c3
32) 4. ♗g5 (or 4. e5)
33) 2. d4
34) 3. ♘c3 (or 3. cxd5, or 3. e5)
35) 3. ♗d3
36) 4. ♘xe4
37) 2. ♘f3
38) 3. ♗g4
39) 3. e3
40) 3. ♗g4
41) 2. ♘f3
42) 3. e3
43) 4. c3
44) 6. O-O (or 6. ♗b2)
45) 3. d4
46) 4. ♘xd4 (or 4. c3, or 4. ♗c4)
47) 5. ♗e3
48) 1. ♗xf7!
49) 2. ♘c3
50) 3. g3 (or 3. f4, or 3. ♗c4)
51) 4. ♕g4
52) 4. ♗g2
53) 2. exd5
54) 3. ♘c3
55) 3. d4
56) 4. d4

Table of contents

Introduction 1
Ruy Lopez (Spanish Game) 2
Italian Game 6
Queen's Gambit 10
Sicilian Defense 14
English Opening 18
Réti Opening 22
King's Indian Attack 26
French Defense 30
Caro-Kann Defense 34
London System 38
Colle System 42
Scotch Game 46
Vienna Game 50
Scandinavian Defense 54
Bishop's Opening 58
Trompowsky Attack 58
Alekhine's Defense 59
Bird's Opening 59
Solutions to Exercises 60

Made in United States
Orlando, FL
13 November 2023